Praying On The Journey With Christ

A Commitment
To Encounter Christ
Through The
Gospel Of John

Richard F. Bansemer

CSS Publishing Company, Inc., Lima, Ohio

PRAYING ON THE JOURNEY WITH CHRIST

Copyright © 1997 by
CSS Publishing Company, Inc.
Lima, Ohio

All rights reserved. No part of this publication may be reproduced in any manner whatsoever without the prior permission of the publisher, except in the case of brief quotations embodied in critical articles and reviews. Inquiries should be addressed to: Permissions, CSS Publishing Company, Inc., P.O. Box 4503, Lima, Ohio 45802-4503.

Scripture quotations are from the *New Revised Standard Version of the Bible*, copyright 1989 by the Division of Christian Education of the National Council of the Churches of Christ in the USA. Used by permission.

Library of Congress Cataloging-in-Publication Data

Bansemer, Richard F., 1940-
   Praying on the journey with Christ : a commitment to encounter Christ through the Gospel of John / Richard F. Bansemer.
     p.   cm.
   ISBN 0-7880-1176-6 (pbk.)
   1. Bible. N.T. John—Devotional literature. 2. Bible. N.T. John—Prayers. I. Title.
BS2615.4.B36   1998
242'.5—dc21   97-39506
                                                                                         CIP

This book is available in the following formats, listed by ISBN:
   0-7880-1176-6   Book
   0-7880-1177-4   IBM 3 1/2
   0-7880-1178-2   MAC
   0-7880-1179-0   Sermon Prep

PRINTED IN U.S.A.

*Pray in the Spirit at all times in
every prayer and supplication.*
(Ephesians 6:18)

*To Mary Ann, my wife,
who prays these prayers
with gladness.*

TABLE OF CONTENTS

Introduction	9
1. Life, Word, Light, Darkness *John 1:1-5*	11
2. Sent *John 1:6-9*	14
3. In, Not Of, The World *John 1:10-13*	16
4. Becoming Less *John 1:14-18*	18
5. Wilderness *John 1:19-28*	20
6. Making God Glad *John 1:29-34*	22
7. Wading In Deeper *John 1:35-51*	24
8. Christ In The Kitchen *John 2:1-12*	26
9. Grace Place *John 2:13-22*	28
10. Miracle Watchers *John 2:23-25*	30
11. Countless Quizzes *John 3:1-15*	32
12. Loving The World *John 3:16*	35
13. Bleaching The Darkest Dark *John 3:17-21*	37
14. Being God's Beloved *John 3:22-36*	39
15. The Will To Listen *John 4:1-42*	41
16. Doing Love *John 4:43-54*	45
17. Saying "Yes" To Healing *John 5:1-18*	47
18. Judgment *John 5:19-30*	50

19.	Pretending To Want God *John 5:31-47*	53
20.	Running To The Mountain *John 6:1-15*	56
21.	Storms And Calm *John 6:16-21*	59
22.	Love Hunger *John 6:22-34*	61
23.	Eternal Bread *John 6:35-40*	65
24.	Love Power *John 6:41-59*	67
25.	Beyond Flesh *John 6:60-71*	70
26.	Beyond Gentle Love *John 7:1-24*	73
27.	Christ In Others *John 7:25-36*	77
28.	Living Water *John 7:37-52*	80
29.	Second Chance *John 8:1-11*	83
30.	Heavenly Father *John 8:12-30*	86
31.	Heirs *John 8:31-38*	89
32.	Using Faith Forever *John 8:39-59*	91
33.	Getting The Mud Out *John 9:1-12*	94
34.	Eyes Earthward *John 9:13-41*	97
35.	Known By Name *John 10:1-10*	100
36.	Slipping Over Cliffs *John 10:11-21*	102
37.	Never Alone *John 10:22-42*	105
38.	Be The Light *John 11:1-16*	108

39. Opening Death's Dark Eyes *John 11:17-27*	111
40. Cry For Us *John 11:28-44*	113
41. Any One Of Us *John 11:45-57*	116
42. Time At His Feet *John 12:1-8*	119
43. Being Died For By The Messiah *John 12:9-26*	122
44. Off Balance, But Pious? *John 12:27-43*	126
45. Gift From The Father *John 12:44-50*	129
46. Lord Of The Washbasin *John 13:1-20*	131
47. Love And Difficult Times *John 13:21-35*	134
48. Winning Us Back *John 13:36-38*	137
49. Enjoy The Father *John 14:1-7*	139
50. Leaving Questions Behind *John 14:8-14*	141
51. Covered *John 14:15-24*	144
52. A Greater Sacrifice *John 14:25-31*	147
53. For The Sake Of Fruit *John 15:1-11*	149
54. Friends *John 15:12-17*	152
55. Hardship As Service *John 15:18—16:4a*	155
56. The Sin Of Unbelief *John 16:4b-15*	158
57. All Doubts Will Vanish *John 16:16-33*	161
58. Together Forever *John 17:1-5*	164

59. God-Esteem *John 17:6-19*	166
60. Team Effort *John 17:20-26*	169
61. For The Father And Us *John 18:1-14*	172
62. Little Matters That Mattered *John 18:15-27*	175
63. Membership In Another World *John 18:28-40*	178
64. Looking At Us With Love *John 19:1-7*	181
65. No Decision At All *John 19:8-16a*	183
66. King Jesus *John 19:16b-25a*	186
67. Let Death Come, Lord Jesus *John 19:25b-27*	188
68. Accomplished *John 19:28-30*	191
69. Blood And Water *John 19:31-37*	194
70. Cemetery *John 19:38-42*	197
71. Walking Away Bewildered *John 20:1-10*	200
72. Name Calling *John 20:11-18*	203
73. The Good News Of Forgiveness *John 20:19-23*	206
74. Messiah *John 20:24-29*	209
75. A Thank You For John *John 20:30, 31*	212
76. When Others Are Around *John 21:1-14*	213
77. One On One *John 21:15-19*	216
78. We Will *John 21:20-25*	219

INTRODUCTION

No other Gospel, and therefore, no other book in the world, provokes as much desire and need for prayer as the Gospel of John.

The Gospel of John is a mysterious biography, a profound contemplation, a challenging discovery of the presence of another life among us.

In the prayers that follow, you, the pray-er, are invited and encouraged to use these prayers as springboards into deeper thoughts than what the prayers themselves have been able to confess. Blocks of silence should occur naturally many times in the prayer. Letting silence happen is prayer. There is no benefit in hurried prayer. The prayers are best prayed in sequence, one after another, following John's skillfully prepared gospel.

These prayers are devotional and intended for individual use. The first person "I" is used, especially in the beginning of the book. Sometimes a prayer will shift from the singular "I" to the plural "we." As my own struggle and sin is spoken in prayer, it is done knowing that a flawed faith is obvious. These prayers are not attempts to demonstrate piety or to teach theology. These prayers are confessions, queries, and one-time meditative thoughts on the Word as written by John. It was a profound surprise to me that the "I" became less and less useful as the prayers evolved. "We" is used much more frequently toward the end of the book.

At first this book was titled *A Pray-er Provoked By The Gospel Of John*. Then the title of the book had a double meaning. The "prayer" provoked by John was more than the written words found in the pages that followed. The pray-er was you and me, in the act of praying, struggling with the God of Jesus, revealed in John, whom Jesus constantly named "Father."

The prayers were written for my own journey somewhat reluctantly and always hopefully. They were written for myself, but with the idea that someone might be overhearing the words, and be able to pray along from another perspective. These prayers are shared for our spiritual journeys together, both with the certainty that God, through prayer, will show us much that we've missed in our daily lives, and with the expectation that our wills, the core of our beings, will begin a necessary and radical lifelong transformation. Prayer is mostly for our own sake, but God dearly loves it.

Some people like to have a disciplined schedule for prayer, others do not. Please feel free to miss a day or more without feeling the pressure of catching up or being "behind."

I wish to thank my wife, Mary Ann, for encouragement and proofreading through the years these prayers were written. Also, appreciation is extended to Connie Seddon for her editing and subtle observations. She wrote: "I loved these prayers. They speak to the inner heart, as does the Gospel of John. The voice is intimate, conversational, and teaches without calling attention to the fact. The prayers look inward, but keep God outside the self and avoid making God 'soft.' They capture our uncertainty and ambivalence, and yet convey a sense of deep peace and inner confidence ... This is a tremendous gift."

1. LIFE, WORD, LIGHT, DARKNESS

John 1:1-5

In the beginning was the Word, and the Word was with God, and the Word was God. He was in the beginning with God. All things came into being through him, and without him not one thing came into being. What has come into being in him was life, and the life was the light of all people. The light shines in the darkness, and the darkness did not overcome it.

COMMENTARY

Three times each, the words "Word" and "being" appear in the text above. Twice each, the following words appear: "beginning," "life," "light," and "darkness."

Obviously, John is taking us right to the beginning of "things." God is already there, and no thought is given to the beginning of God, since God has no beginning. No real God could ever have a beginning or an ending. John expects us to understand this naturally. As we enter into prayer over the beginning of every "thing," it is important to know to whom we are talking. At the very least, it is God and the Word, who are one, yet separate and distinct from one another. Both God and Word are referred to as "he," which means that "Word" is something more than what God did or does. The Word is God, and both Word and God are addressed therefore as "he" or "you" in the prayers that follow.

PRAYER 1

Heavenly Father, heavenly Word, speak to me as once you spoke to a void. Out of nothing you called and created everything, by syllables alone. Come, Lord, into this void of myself, and speak to me that I may become your person, and in becoming, bring you joy.

Lord, even as I speak these words I hold back, afraid that you might respond. I am afraid of all that would mean. I am afraid of what you might require of me. I am afraid of what it would do to my life.

There, I've already said it: "MY life." How quickly I've claimed as mine what you've created as your own. How quickly I've seen my life on top of that list of your creations. This is my darkness, Lord, and I confess my darkness to you as sin. Only your life and light can overcome it.

Lord, John's words about the beginning fill me with as many questions as answers. How does the relationship between you as the Word and you as God work? Are my thoughts in word-form acceptable to you, the Word? Already, I hear you saying, "Don't pray like this ... don't try to complicate our communication ... don't philosophize with me."

What, then, Lord, shall I do? Shall I sit and wait for you to speak? Yes, I know that is quite acceptable to you, so help me do it. Help me read about you and then give you time to speak. Help me to be open to your presence, that you may tell me about life, and Word, and light, and darkness.

About life you say, "It is my gift, and I sustain it every moment." Thank you, Lord, for this moment with you. Thank you for all that comes before my mind as additional gifts to the gift of life. Thank you, Lord, for mind and heart, lungs and senses, and friends with the same gifts. Thank you for this moment. All life is of a moment.

About the Word, you say, "He is my presence, always speaking, always talking, but heard only by those quiet enough to listen." Lord, you know that the noises of this world are intense, as are the noises of my own mind. Help me come to quiet that I may hear your still, small voice. Help me discern that the voice is real ... from a being, your being, your presence. Lord, your Word is not an echo of a voice spoken long ago, still rolling about in space, but evidence of your presence with me now ... alive, working, molding, doing.

About the light you say, "I am more than brightness. I am the way to walk, the path of joy, the purpose for your being." Lord, like many others, I claim to want a life of purpose, a life of meaning. Walk with me all day, all night, and help me see the people I meet, and the events that occur, as opportunities to see your light at work.

About the darkness you say, "It is darker than black. It is the power that would swallow you up, if I let it. It is more powerful than your own life, your own will, your own sin. It is a terror more horrible than annihilation, and an enemy more committed than you are to me at this moment." Lord, I know it, and I am sorry. I know that the darkness presses in on me and all others. I can feel him. I am afraid of him ... much more than I am afraid of you, for I know he wants me for evil's sake. I see much evidence of him in my life, and I want him out.

Yes, I hear you say, "Not entirely ... not entirely do I want him out."

Lord, why do I hang on to the darkness within myself so tightly? Why won't I let you have me? Why am I more obsessed with the darkness within me than I am with the darkness of the world? What am I afraid of losing? Am I afraid of the world, too?

Lord, heavenly God, heavenly Word, I recognize that I shall never be all yours if I am left only to my own power to become yours. If possible, gently lead me to yourself; but if gentleness will not accomplish the task, then work with me another way, and give me courage and wisdom to let you.

Finally, Lord, John reminds me that "all things come into being through you." Come into my being, that through your being, through your light, and through your life, and by your Word, I shall not be overcome by darkness. Amen.

2. SENT

John 1:6-9
There was a man sent from God, whose name was John. He came as a witness to testify to the light, so that all might believe through him. He himself was not the light, but he came to testify to the light. The true light, which enlightens everyone, was coming into the world.

COMMENTARY
John the Baptist is introduced in this passage of Scripture as one who was sent from God to tell about the light that was coming, so that all might believe. He was a man with a mission, working by faith, for he was testifying to what he had not yet seen.

PRAYER 2
Heavenly light, true light, sender of John the Baptist to those who want to shine within like a candle in a lamp, how am I to believe this man if he is not the light himself? What did he know of the Christ who was coming? What are his credentials?

Lord, I am very suspicious of witnesses. Their imaginations are often better than their memories. Their motives are more suspect than their message. I have been barraged by false witnesses all my life. I check others out, Lord, and they check me out, too. I look for secret agendas and ulterior motives. I keep track of others' accomplishments, degrees, and privileges. I don't trust just anyone anymore.

I'm glad that John the Baptist didn't have to say that he was sent by you, for that would make him harder to believe. I'm glad that it was said *about* him, not by him. More than anything, though, I'm glad that you sent him. I am glad that you send.

John's task, Lord, seemed doomed to fail from the start. I would not have wanted his job. It seems to me as though you shorted him on power. He had to witness with vigor to what he had not yet seen. At least, Lord, he could talk about "light" to people who knew what a dark night was all about! Today, in this neon world of electric lights and city streets, his job would be impossible.

Lord, you sent John, a mere human being, to do holy work. You sent him out and away from the traffic of the day, and expected the rest of us to listen ... to look for an approaching light. You gave him a duty and a message about the light, but you made him work by faith. You made him work in the dark ... and in the wilderness.

Thank you, Lord, for John. Thank you for gifting him with enough faith to keep on track, even in the dark, and among dark souls. Thank you for using one of us mortals to do immortal work.

Lord, help me learn and be about what you've sent me to do for you, not so dramatically as John, of course, but with every bit the same credentials as a child of your own rearing and redeeming. Amen.

3. IN, NOT OF, THE WORLD

John 1:10-13

He was in the world, and the world came into being through him; yet the world did not know him. He came to what was his own, and his own people did not accept him. But to all who received him, who believed in his name, he gave power to become children of God, who were born, not of blood or of the will of the flesh or of the will of man, but of God.

COMMENTARY

Who would not want to recognize an artist who has painted a great painting, a musician who has written a great symphony, or an author who has penned a great novel? The earth's creator hung out our blue sunlit sphere, suspended in space with the only known life forms in the universe, then came and walked on earth as one of us. "He was in the world ... yet the world did not know him."

Both the recognition and nonrecognition of God among his people has familial consequences. A power is given to those who notice who Jesus is. God's people are given a "power" unlike any other power on earth. We are given the power to be a child again, and the power to know that being a child of God is greater than any other earthly power.

PRAYER 3

Lord, Jesus Christ, to be your Father's child is my highest aspiration. May I want to be his child more than every other want.

Even as I pray these words, I understand some of the consequences if you grant me the high status of child. If your God is my Father, and the Father of all others, then all of us together are brothers and sisters in a world of horrific imbalances, and I confess to having more than my fair share of goods. Help me share my abundance with all my brothers and sisters. Teach me how to live with less, willingly, so that I may be more in love with you and the rest of our family.

Heavenly Father, help me see this day like a day from my first childhood: a day full of wonder, full of surprise, and full of mystery.

Help me explore it with as much delight and glee as I did when I first discovered how wonderful this earth-place is. May I sense your hand still shaping and sustaining all the life I witness about me this day. In so doing, may I learn to care for the earth, because I care for you.

Yet, Lord, I do not want to worship the creation, but you alone, the Creator. I do not want your work of art to be the object of my affection. I only want you to be my Father, and for me to be your child. I want you to want me to be your child forever.

Lord, keep me from over-romanticizing this beautiful earth, to the point where my love for it blinds me to the real problems on it. Help me keep the beauty of the whole earth in balance with the horror of the pain that happens here.

Lord, when you come to me and I do not recognize you, come again and again. Do not let me not see you. Shake me awake or fill me with enough guilt, shame, love, or homesickness for you, that I must open my eyes to see you near. Amen.

4. BECOMING LESS

John 1:14-18
And the Word became flesh and dwelt among us, full of grace and truth; we have beheld his glory, glory as of the only Son from the Father. (John bore witness to him, and cried, "This was he of whom I said, 'He who comes after me ranks before me, for he was before me.'") And from his fullness we have all received, grace upon grace. For the law was given through Moses; grace and truth came through Jesus Christ. No one has ever seen God; the only Son, who is in the bosom of the Father, he has made him known. (RSV)

COMMENTARY

This text, often used at Christmastime, is filled with the word "grace." Grace is the one and only motive God has for coming to us. Because love itself is irrational, trying to understand God's coming is as preposterous as trying to understand the infinite with a finite mind. This "grace upon grace" is the cornerstone from which God operates. No one explains the cornerstone. All we can do is give thanks that it is there, build upon it, and be glad that we are close to the Father's heart of grace.

PRAYER 4

Lord God, your incarnation, your becoming flesh among us as a man named Jesus, is a mystery so profound as to confound all logical thinking. You became less for the sake of love.

I cannot imagine, Heavenly Father, ever asking my only son or my only daughter to become less for me. And, if you were to ask me, and even if I understood why it was necessary to become a lesser being, I think I would insist upon a few loopholes, a couple of exit points, in case I changed my mind, in case the world said "no" to my arrival.

Becoming flesh, Lord, was not just a step "down." It was a step out of glory and away from your home. It was the acceptance of a mission so unlikely to succeed that it might be called "reckless."

There were too many prophecies to fulfill, and too many contradictory ideas of what a Messiah would do and look like.

Lord Jesus Christ, I'm glad you did it. Without your witness, your teachings, your life, what would I know about you and your Father's intention for me as a human being? What would anyone know of the purposes of earth life? Who would guess that there is more life to come?

Lord Jesus Christ, thank you for risking yourself for me. Please, do not measure the worthiness of your coming solely by my response, else you would have to doubt the cost. Instead, imagine what I, and millions of others, would be like without your coming, without your "grace upon grace," without your love gifts upon love gifts. Though I am not good at being your person, without your coming I would only care about today, this world, and myself.

Lord Jesus Christ, you always point to the Father. So close you are to him, it makes me want to know him also. You alone "make him known." You alone make me wonder if being made in your image is the same as being "bone of your bone, and flesh of your flesh." As I seek to journey with you through the days of my life, may I never forget the goal of knowing not only you, but also your Father who sent you ... your Father who sent you for me. Amen.

5. WILDERNESS

John 1:19-28

This is the testimony of John, when the Jews sent priests and Levites from Jerusalem to ask him, "Who are you?" He confessed, he did not deny, but confessed, "I am not the Messiah." And they asked him, "What then? Are you Elijah?" He said, "I am not." "Are you the prophet?" And he answered, "No." Then they said to him, "Who are you? Let us have an answer for those who sent us. What do you say about yourself?" He said, "I am the voice of one crying in the wilderness, 'Make straight the way of the Lord,' as the prophet Isaiah said."

Now they had been sent from the Pharisees. They asked him, "Why then are you baptizing, if you are neither the Messiah, nor Elijah, nor the prophet?" John answered them, "I baptize with water. Among you stands one whom you do not know, the one who is coming after me; I am not worthy to untie the thong of his sandal." This took place in Bethany across the Jordan where John was baptizing.

COMMENTARY

John the Baptist wants to tell the people what to do in order to get ready for the coming of Christ, the Messiah. His critics did not want to know what to do, but who he, John, was. Again and again they ask him, "Who are you? Are you a prophet? Are you the Messiah? Are you Elijah?" To every question, John the Baptist holds true to his mission, to tell the people what to do to get ready for the coming of God incarnate, God in flesh, God as Jesus.

After the question of the identity of John had been settled in the minds of his questioners, they are curious enough to ask, "Why, then, are you baptizing?" John clearly differentiates between the kind of baptism he is called upon to do by the washing of oneself and the kind of baptism in the Spirit that will come when one whose shoes he is unworthy to untie appears. This distinction in baptisms is as different as a patient's scrub-down before surgery, and the actual opening of the patient's body for the sake of restoring health. John's baptism is preparatory. Baptism in the Spirit is a spiritual transplant.

PRAYER 5

Lord, you know that my heart is hidden in a wilderness, every bit as remote and wild as the wilderness of John the Baptist. I have hidden myself deeply in the woods, so that others cannot affect me, so that I can avoid unpleasant confrontations with myself, so that even you must search for me every day in a forever game of hide-and-seek. I am fascinated with my own ability to hide from you, others, and myself. At least, I am often fascinated with what I think are successful attempts to hide from you, the "hound of heaven."

Your servant, John, told us to open up a way for you to get through to us — a straight way for the coming of the Lord. You know those things that make me reveal my hiding place. You, Lord, when you are near, make me want to explode like a child hiding from a parent playing hide-and-seek. You, Lord, say, "Here I come" and "I'm getting close!"

After we have played this game a few times, Lord, you expect more from me than admission of your nearness. You not only begin to surprise me with your presence, but you also speak words to my will. You ask me to wash up and get ready for work. You tell me to get ready for a fuller measure of your presence. You tell me you want to surprise me with your presence, eat with me at my table, and feed me with your own body. You tell me that you are going to use me in work beyond my understanding. You tell me you are going to infiltrate my life, take over my will, and transform me into your agent.

I am immensely satisfied with the honor. I am terrorized by the magnitude of what you might require of me to be faithful. You know I am not so brave. You know how I hate to be wrong. You know I think I would want to do anything you ask, but I like to have more to go on than faith. Yes, Lord, this is a confession.

Lord, if John the Baptist was unworthy to untie your sandals, the rest of us are in one terrible predicament! He knew less of you than we do, yet believed. Thank you for his example of faith. I only wish I didn't know what happened to him for being faithful.

Increase my courage, Lord. Transform my will. Help me have less fear of silver platters with severed heads, than the wilderness of living without you. Amen.

6. MAKING GOD GLAD

John 1:29-34

The next day he saw Jesus coming toward him and declared, "Here is the Lamb of God who takes away the sin of the world! This is he of whom I said, 'After me comes a man who ranks ahead of me because he was before me.' I myself did not know him; but I came baptizing with water for this reason, that he might be revealed to Israel." And John testified, "I saw the Spirit descending from heaven like a dove and it remained on him. I myself did not know him, but the one who sent me to baptize with water said to me, 'He on whom you see the Spirit descend and remain is the one who baptizes with the Holy Spirit.' And I myself have seen and have testified that this is the Son of God."

COMMENTARY

"Here is the Lamb ... this is the Son of God." Between these two phrases, the first phrase talking about the Lamb, and the last phrase talking about the Son (both of which are "of God"), it is the Holy Spirit that is most operative in this passage. The work of the Holy Spirit in this passage is one of identifying the Messiah. The Spirit is described as descending like a dove, remaining on him like some creature from space, but with a true homing instinct.

The Holy Spirit, obviously, belongs with the Lamb of God, the Son of God. To be baptized by the Holy Spirit is to be touched and tapped by the Lamb of God, the Son of God, and the Spirit of God. To be baptized by the Holy Spirit is to be surrounded by God, from whom there is no escape, and to rejoice in that captivity.

PRAYER 6

Lord Holy Spirit, sometimes I've imagined it was you who brushed by me, like some furtive butterfly on its erratic path. I would be like Saint Francis of Assisi, if only I could.

Sometimes I've wished you would light on me like a dove, and someone like John the Baptist would see it and announce its beauty.

I don't blame you, Lord, if you are as afraid of me as butterflies and birds are. I am a fickle person. Today I want you near. Tomorrow may be another story.

What I'm really asking for is a friendly, nice relationship, but not necessarily a deep one. Like the gentle butterfly and the timid bird, I don't mind your being near, or even lighting on me, but entering within, becoming a part of me, and changing the way I think and live is quite another matter. Oh, Lord, I like to watch. I like to see you in living things. I do not like to listen to you. I do not like to change.

Lord Holy Spirit, of what am I afraid? Why won't I listen? If I were able to listen, would you enter into me in fullness? Do you only come to ready hearts, open hearts, vulnerable hearts? I think so.

When John saw you, Lord, he knew who you were. He knew that your task was more than flitting about like a butterfly. In the wilderness he had listened to the heavenly voice intently. He had listened, so he knew you when he saw you.

Lord Holy Spirit, come into my life every day, reminding me of my baptism. Come, not just for the peace and joy that you bring, nor even for the power that you are. Rather, come to me, for I am lonely without you, and I want to learn how to bring you joy and make you glad. Amen.

7. WADING IN DEEPER

John 1:35-51

The next day John again was standing with two of his disciples, and as he watched Jesus walk by, he exclaimed, "Look, here is the Lamb of God!" The two disciples heard him say this, and they followed Jesus. When Jesus turned and saw them following, he said to them, "What are you looking for?" They said to him, "Rabbi" (which translated means Teacher), "where are you staying?" He said to them, "Come and see." They came and saw where he was staying, and they remained with him that day. It was about four o'clock in the afternoon. One of the two who heard John speak and followed him was Andrew, Simon Peter's brother. He first found his brother Simon and said to him, "We have found the Messiah" (which is translated Anointed). He brought Simon to Jesus, who looked at him and said "You are Simon son of John. You are to be called Cephas" (which is translated Peter).

The next day Jesus decided to go to Galilee. He found Philip and said to him, "Follow me." Now Philip was from Bethsaida, the city of Andrew and Peter. Philip found Nathanael and said to him, "We have found him about whom Moses in the law and also the prophets wrote, Jesus son of Joseph from Nazareth." Nathanael said to him, "Can anything good come out of Nazareth?" Philip said to him, "Come and see." When Jesus saw Nathanael coming toward him, he said to him, "Here is truly an Israelite in whom there is no deceit!" Nathanael asked him, "Where did you get to know me?" Jesus answered, "I saw you under the fig tree before Philip called you." Nathanael replied, "Rabbi, you are the Son of God! You are the King of Israel!" Jesus answered, "Do you believe because I told you that I saw you under the fig tree? You will see greater things than these." And he said to him, "Very truly, I tell you, you will see heaven opened and the angels of God ascending and descending upon the Son of Man."

COMMENTARY

The first recorded words of Jesus in the Gospel of John are: "What are you looking for?"

Jesus was being followed by Andrew and one other disciple of John the Baptist. John had revealed the identity of Jesus to the two men as "the Lamb of God."

One contact led to another, and by the end of the passage, Jesus had at least four disciples, and probably five (if the unnamed other disciple with Andrew was John, the author of this Gospel).

The promise of Jesus at the beginning of these disciples' discipleship is that they will see great things, and he refers to himself as "the Son of Man."

PRAYER 7

Lamb of God, Son of Man, how quickly you enlisted disciples. I wonder why John the Baptist wasn't one of the originals? Perhaps his own calling as preparer was every bit as sacred as the call to the twelve who followed.

Lord, I often feel like I'm tagging along behind you, like Andrew and friend, seeing where you're going, before showing too much interest. I am a curious, cautious follower. Sometimes I'm not even sure it's you I'm following.

I'd like to follow when you're planning to do some miracle. I'd rather wait outside if you ever plan to cleanse a temple again.

I'd like to follow you and hear you teach and preach pure poetry from a mountaintop, or from an offshore boat. I'd rather not get into any arguments with people asking hostile questions.

I'd like to be in the upper room and be among those who drink from your cup and eat from your loaf. I'd rather not have to try to stay awake in Gethsemane after supper.

I'd love to meet you at the empty tomb on Sunday morning. I'd rather not be at Golgotha Friday afternoon.

Yes, Lord, I'm not sure how close I want to follow and which of these are the "greater things" you told Nathanael he would see.

I am forever wanting you to be a warm, wooly, and passive innocent little lamb — my Lamb of God. Unlike a lamb, you are forever being bold, demanding, unyielding, sure of the Father's will for you and us, truly a Son of Man, the Son of God.

Lamb of God, Son of Man, how persistently you seek to make us perfect lambs of God. I try not to know that perfect lambs are made for sacrifice. Amen.

8. CHRIST IN THE KITCHEN

John 2:1-12

On the third day there was a wedding in Cana of Galilee, and the mother of Jesus was there. Jesus and his disciples had also been invited to the wedding. When the wine gave out, the mother of Jesus said to him, "They have no wine." And Jesus said to her, "Woman, what concern is that to you and to me? My hour has not yet come." His mother said to the servants, "Do whatever he tells you." Now standing there were six stone water jars for the Jewish rites of purification, each holding twenty or thirty gallons. Jesus said to them, "Fill the jars with water." And they filled them to the brim. He said to them, "Now draw some out, and take it to the chief steward." So they took it. When the steward tasted the water that had become wine, and did not know where it came from (though the servants who had drawn the water knew), the steward called the bridegroom and said to him, "Everyone serves the good wine first, and then the inferior wine after the guests have become drunk. But you have kept the good wine until now." Jesus did this, the first of his signs, in Cana of Galilee, and revealed his glory; and his disciples believed in him.

After this he went down to Capernaum with his mother, his brothers, and his disciples; and they remained there a few days.

COMMENTARY

Twice John tells us exactly where Jesus did the first of his signs. People and places make ministry real. Jesus' ministry is grounded in real places, real people, and real events. There is little need to speculate about a phantom God, with no more substance than a wisp of smoke. The wedding was as real as the kitchen, the six stone water jars, the bride, the groom, the guests, and Cana in Galilee.

PRAYER 8

Lord Jesus Christ, you seem to have been forced to begin your ministry before you were ready. Like a mother robin, your mother seems to have pushed you, ever so gently, into the public arena.

I wonder where and how you expected your signals to begin? It is surprising to see you caring about such a mundane problem — a matter of inconsequence when set against the big problems of the world. It is surprising to see you and your disciples at the wedding as invited guests. Surely, you were too busy to come. Surely, there were far greater needs to attend to.

Lord, how am I to understand what you want from me, except to try to be where the need is greatest? Yet you simply took care of a little problem, as though that were an important enough matter on which to spend a rare miracle.

You made a lot of wine, Lord. Such abundance. Perhaps miracles aren't as rare as I suppose. Perhaps they are appropriate at places where the need isn't always critical.

But you see what this does? It makes it impossible to know when to expect a miracle. When is one due? Why does one person "get" a miracle when he wants one, and someone else doesn't?

No one really asked for a miracle, yet that was the solution you chose to solve the problem. I choose that too, Lord, but I can't make it happen. I don't have your power.

You knew, of course, that once you did a miracle things would never be the same for you again. You would be in demand. You would be noticed and talked about. (How did you do it, Lord? How are physical things under your control, just like spiritual things?)

I know that's not the point. I know that this is a diversion from seeing you as hospitable — doing graciously what only you could do, suggesting that I do what only I can do in any situation.

Lord, like you, help me to give more than necessary. Teach me the art of hospitality. Give me such an interest in others, that their special moments become special to me, too. And when I am successful, at a real time, in a real place, with real people, may I remember that I learned this grace from you. Amen.

9. GRACE PLACE

John 2:13-22

The Passover of the Jews was near, and Jesus went up to Jerusalem. In the temple he found people selling cattle, sheep, and doves, and the money changers seated at their tables. Making a whip of cords, he drove all of them out of the temple, both the sheep and the cattle. He also poured out the coins of the money changers and overturned their tables. He told those who were selling the doves, "Take these things out of here! Stop making my Father's house a marketplace!" His disciples remembered that it was written, "Zeal for your house will consume me." The Jews then said to him, "What sign can you show us for doing this?" Jesus answered them, "Destroy this temple, and in three days I will raise it up." The Jews then said, "This temple has been under construction for forty-six years, and you will raise it up in three days?" But he was speaking of the temple of his body. After he was raised from the dead, his disciples remembered that he had said this; and they believed the scripture and the word that Jesus had spoken.

COMMENTARY

Jesus seems to continue to act spontaneously — even impulsively — as he purges the temple. This passage is the first time God is named "Father" in John, and it is interesting to note that it follows immediately upon the miracle involving his mother. Very deliberately, Jesus is beginning to show the difference between earthly parenthood and godly Fatherhood.

Not only is the use of "Father" a sort of play on words, so is the word "temple." Some of us can see only with earthly eyes (a stone temple — a mortal parent), but Jesus makes us think of more holy concepts, where all bodies are temples, and our creator Father resides both in heaven and with us.

PRAYER 9

Lord Jesus Christ, your Father's house is still a marketplace. We have built churches by the thousands to serve ourselves and our families. We have, in your name, taken very good care of ourselves, seeking to meet every need from birth to death.

Lord Jesus, as members of the marketplace church, taking care of all our personal needs, are we also members of your Father's house, conversing with him about his way and world? How are we to grow beyond the lethargic comforts of our home church to the excitement and experience of meeting you in strange places, doing wonderful things? I feel that lure of adventure to go with you into a new and deeper relationship, even as I caution myself, saying, "Careful, this could be uncomfortable. This could be dangerous ... wild."

Lord, I see you drawing back your whip that scattered the temple animals, and I wonder if I am only one of them, marked for sacrifice, too frightened and dumb to know that you would free me from certain death. I see the plentiful oats and barley that taste so good and make me fat, but know that all my days are numbered short if I live in a feeding lot. I see my value as part of the herd, and I like the looks of those who praise my worth, yet know that they would sacrifice me, for their own sake.

Who am I, Lord, a sheep marked for slaughter, or a child of your grace? I know which of these I am, Lord, even if this earthly body-temple of mine is destroyed. I know you are my Father and will raise me up to meet you face to face. Amen.

10. MIRACLE WATCHERS

John 2:23-25
When he was in Jerusalem during the Passover festival, many believed in his name because they saw the signs that he was doing. But Jesus on his part would not entrust himself to them, because he knew all people and needed no one to testify about anyone; for he himself knew what was in everyone.

COMMENTARY

The people who believed in Jesus because of his miracles missed his essence, and Jesus was unimpressed with their "belief." Jesus was more than intuitive. He knew another person without need of recommendation from anyone else. He was already what he will be at the end of time. He was, is, and shall be judge. He could not, cannot, and will not be fooled. Most significantly, he will not "entrust himself" to untrustworthy believers.

PRAYER 10

Lord Jesus Christ, I can't help but wonder how much better I would know you if I were more trustworthy. My own motives for loving you are more complex than the circuits of my mind, and less pure than the rainwaters on a busy city street. How will you ever sort out and use my frail and incomplete trust of you? How can I ever know you more if I must be more trustworthy? By my own weakness I am undone.

The miracles you performed created great interest in you, yet you would not accept faith based on signs. It's as though you were saying, "I have all things under my authority. Here's proof. But don't believe in me for this reason."

We all like signs, Lord. We all ask for an occasional miracle. By the mere thought of approaching you with an impossible problem, we glorify your name. We recognize your power.

Still, there nag these words about you: "He would not entrust himself to them." We who need some proof from time to time, some reassurance that you're still busy taking care of things, come off as second-class believers. If we hope for a first-class miracle, we seem to make ourselves unworthy of you.

Lord, there are those who came to you with big problems, for whom you granted a miracle and whom you used as examples of faithfulness. What is the difference between them and those others who marvelled at your power? Is it because the watchers stayed on the outside, objectively evaluating your style, without really coming into faith? Is it because you don't want watchers who are mere critics of your way, but rather followers who will risk something precious for you?

Lord, I confess that I have often looked to you for quick and easy solutions to my problems. I confess I've wanted miracles for miracles' sake. My motives for coming to you are often selfish, and always less than holy.

I look for the day, Lord, in fear, but also in hope, when you entrust more of yourself to me. May I be able to handle, with your grace, what you give of yourself to me, so that neither you nor I am ashamed of my growth in faithfulness. Amen.

11. COUNTLESS QUIZZES

John 3:1-15

Now there was a Pharisee named Nicodemus, a leader of the Jews. He came to Jesus by night and said to him, "Rabbi, we know that you are a teacher who has come from God; for no one can do these signs that you do apart from the presence of God." Jesus answered him, "Very truly, I tell you, no one can see the kingdom of God without being born from above." Nicodemus said to him, "How can anyone be born after having grown old? Can one enter a second time into the mother's womb and be born?" Jesus answered, "Very truly, I tell you, no one can enter the kingdom of God without being born of water and spirit. What is born of the flesh is flesh, and what is born of the Spirit is spirit. Do not be astonished that I said to you, 'You must be born from above.' The wind blows where it chooses, and you hear the sound of it, but you do not know where it comes from or where it goes. So it is with everyone who is born of the Spirit." Nicodemus said to him, "How can these things be?" Jesus answered him, "Are you a teacher of Israel and yet you do not understand these things?"

"Very truly, I tell you, we speak of what we know and testify to what we have seen; yet you do not receive our testimony. If I have told you about earthly things and you do not believe, how can you believe if I tell you about heavenly things? No one has ascended into heaven except the one who descended from heaven, the Son of Man. And just as Moses lifted up the serpent in the wilderness, so must the Son of Man be lifted up, that whoever believes in him may have eternal life."

COMMENTARY

We owe a lot to inquirers like Nicodemus, who have enough curiosity to ask spiritual questions at the right moment, and to remember the answers for the rest of us. Since only Jesus and Nicodemus were involved in this nighttime discourse, one of them had to report the event. Nicodemus was probably the one who shared the experience with others, since he was the one in search of faith and was likely to be forever impressed.

The concepts contained in the conversation between Jesus and Nicodemus have been topics of debate through the ages. We know what it is to be "born of the flesh," for that is our current experience. But to be "born from above" or "born of the Spirit" is to be born of God, and the details of this second birth are not all that definite. Since there is no overt physical evidence, we hardly know how to measure the reality of such a birth.

The clues of spiritual birth are vague to us because they are other-worldly, and require interpretation and accomplishment in history. So, when Jesus states that the Son of Man has to be lifted up, like a serpent in the wilderness, one has to know about Moses lifting up the snake on a pole to spare his people from poisonous snake bites. Jesus takes no offense to his own approaching crucifixion on a tree being compared to the snake on a pole. Both of them save lives, the first in an historical physical sense, and the second in a forever spiritual sense.

The test for Nicodemus is to believe in what has not yet historically occurred (the crucifixion), even if it's so veiled and incomprehensible as to be impossible to fully imagine. The test for us is also to believe in what has not yet occurred, namely the second coming of Christ in all his glory, with our own resurrection as part of his victory over death.

PRAYER 11

Lord, was Nicodemus attracted to you because of the signs you did or because of what you said about "heavenly things"?

Most of the world doesn't believe in heavenly things, except as being unrelated to our daily living on earth. I spend little time thinking of you, sensing your presence, trying to make contact. I, like most others I know, make "daily bread" instead. What's worse, I often try to use what I think is spiritual to get more of the physical — more "bread." Like a child trying to trick a parent into getting something, I pretend to love you.

What am I after when I do that? Am I really as transparent as I think I am, or do I, occasionally, have better than bad motives in talking with you? Certainly, even if my prayer is filled with sin, it is still directed to you. And if I sense the unworthiness of my prayer, yet pray it anyway, am I not at least hoping that you will bring good out of evil, that you will listen and sort through the obvious selfishness within the words, and find me, your child, asking questions like Nicodemus?

Maybe it's the questions that are the problem, for I know I can hold you back from my inner life by countless quizzes. Is that why you got weary with Nicodemus? Did he just come for information, or did he want you? Was it just explanation he wanted, and answers to questions? Was he like me as a child asking, "Why? Why? Why?" without listening for an answer? Did he not notice to whom he was talking?

Lord, since you are Spirit, if I am to approach you "in Spirit," how can I get beyond mere words to you and thoughts about you? How can I be in your presence without talking — without thinking? How can I let you in close without words, if words are the main vehicle of expression between us?

Yes, Lord, it's true, I've never heard you speak audibly to me ... never. Never so much as a single word, yet I have sensed you listening and answering. How did you do that without words? How did you get into my heart without my hearing you coming, hearing you talking? How did I know it was you?

Lord, help me give you time, when we are together, to talk. Help me give you the freedom to pick the topic first, once in a while. Help me to be open to your presence without conditions, or questions, or needs. Help me be with you. Amen.

12. LOVING THE WORLD

John 3:16
"For God so loved the world that he gave his only Son, so that everyone who believes in him may not perish but may have eternal life."

COMMENTARY

This, the best known verse of Scripture, needs no commentary. It is a primal source of faith to all who believe and among the first of all passages to be committed to memory.

PRAYER 12

Lord God, you loved, therefore, you gave. You loved profusely. You gave extravagantly. You loved the world, and your world makes life possible. You gave your Son, so that life in your world might have joy beyond earth's own experience.

Lord God, you love the world you gave, the Son you gave, and the creatures made in your very own image. You have made it possible for us to know earth life as first life, and life in Christ your Son as full life, forever life, eternal life.

Lord God, you included all of us in your loving, all of us in your giving, though we are all still sinners. You included everyone in your call to the hopeful experience of faith that leads to eternal life. You made the world and all of us in it, and we are all dependent upon you. May we rejoice in your love, your greatness, and your willingness to let us share in the experiences of beauty, love, and life in this physical world.

Lord God, you related us all to one another, so that none of us is less than precious in your eyes, none of us less precious than your only begotten Son. Our highest goal is to know you as our Father, one another as brother and sister, and your world as home. May we never despise the beauty of the physical, the mystery of the Spirit in flesh, your love incarnate in a perfect Son, our Savior, Jesus Christ.

Lord God, keep us from yearning so much for the spiritual that we despise the physical. Open our eyes to see your creative hand in every particle of dust, in every vista in the universe, in every child's wrist that pulses with life in every land. Help us love what you loved and give as you gave. May we enjoy these moments on earth in the flesh until you come with a new life that will be marked forever with marvelous appreciation for this one. Amen.

13. BLEACHING THE DARKEST DARK

John 3:17-21

"Indeed, God did not send the Son into the world to condemn the world, but in order that the world might be saved through him. Those who believe in him are not condemned; but those who do not believe are condemned already, because they have not believed in the name of the only Son of God. And this is the judgment, that the light has come into the world, and people loved darkness rather than light because their deeds were evil. For all who do evil hate the light and do not come to the light, so that their deeds may not be exposed. But those who do what is true come to the light, so that it may be clearly seen that their deeds have been done in God."

COMMENTARY

Jesus continues to explain his mission without revealing to Nicodemus that he is the person through whom God's mission is being accomplished. Soon that will change, and he will clearly identify himself as God's light in the world. However, this concluding statement to Nicodemus is not yet intimate, and one might suppose that Nicodemus has not yet come to faith in Christ. The invitation of Jesus, to have our deeds be done in God, is a major desire of all who do not want to labor in vain. The only way to assure that our deeds are worthwhile is to be persons of faith.

PRAYER 13

Lord Jesus Christ, you talked about God to Nicodemus. You used theological language and ideas. You spoke objectively of God's work for a big world, of his light coming on like floodlights, yet it all seems so impersonal and cosmic. Not until you begin to talk about our love of the darkness, instead of his light, does it begin to dawn that you are that light that is coming into the world, and you are the light not loved. You make light something other than wattage. You are light and you lighten the spirituality of the deeds we do in a physical world. You show us why we do the things we do.

You shine on our souls, and your light is blinding. These words make me worry, Lord. How much faith in you is enough faith in order to be saved? I worry about this because I know that my faith is not pure, not total, not nearly strong enough to feel confident of salvation. If you make salvation dependent upon my faith alone, I cannot attain it. If you bathe me in your pure light, I will be seen as dirty, and my deeds will be seen as a confusion of motives, the sordidness of which I cringe to think about.

Lord, in these admissions, I take no comfort, even knowing that I have only confessed my need of you, my need of a Savior. I want to be a person who loves your light, does deeds in the light, and proudly bears your name, but my trust in you is not enough. I cannot believe in you through my own power. I cannot take comfort in my yearnings. I cannot take comfort in my accomplishments. I cannot take comfort in myself, for I know I am not faithful enough to be saved.

Lord, use my life and work as best you can. I know that I live and work in subdued light, if not in total darkness, most of the time. Use my deeds intended to be a witness to you, and forgive my darkness that doubts their value. Use even my evil deeds for your glory, but keep me from supposing it doesn't matter that I did them.

You have given me life. You use my mortal being as an incarnation of your love. You discredit the darkness that would discourage me. You bleach the darkest dark through the blazing radiance of loving atonement. Amen.

14. BEING GOD'S BELOVED

John 3:22-36
After this Jesus and his disciples went into the Judean countryside, and he spent some time there with them and baptized. John also was baptizing at Aenon near Salim because water was abundant there; and people kept coming and were being baptized — John, of course, had not yet been thrown into prison.

Now a discussion about purification arose between John's disciples and a Jew. They came to John and said to him, "Rabbi, the one who was with you across the Jordan, to whom you testified, here he is baptizing, and all are going to him." John answered, "No one can receive anything except what has been given from heaven. You yourselves are my witnesses that I said, 'I am not the Messiah, but I have been sent ahead of him.' He who has the bride is the bridegroom. The friend of the bridegroom, who stands and hears him, rejoices greatly at the bridegroom's voice. For this reason my joy has been fulfilled. He must increase, but I must decrease."

The one who comes from above is above all; the one who is of the earth belongs to the earth and speaks about earthly things. The one who comes from heaven is above all. He testifies to what he has seen and heard, yet no one accepts his testimony. Whoever has accepted his testimony has certified this, that God is true. He whom God has sent speaks the words of God, for he gives the Spirit without measure. The Father loves the Son and has placed all things in his hands. Whoever believes in the Son has eternal life; whoever disobeys the Son will not see life, but must endure God's wrath.

COMMENTARY

What could have been a power struggle between Jesus and John the Baptist is defused by a magnanimous John. Without a shred of doubt, John knows that his mission is to be "best man" to Christ the bridegroom, and in that role John finds joy. He is an example of perfect faithfulness to his task and genuine expectation for his Lord's coming ministry. His testimony is of one who has seen the Messiah coming after himself, and points to Christ, with boldness, excitement, and conviction.

PRAYER 14

Lord Jesus, John looked forward to your coming with such joy that he had to compare his happiness to that of a best man waiting for his friend's wedding. He looked forward to your arrival and your uniting with humankind, and he did not think that the metaphor of "marriage" was any other than the perfect image to describe your love for us. You take no offense at becoming one with us. You take no offense at having your love and devotion consummated in a marriage. You know how weak and frail and helpless we are. Nevertheless, you unite with us to make us who we are.

Lord Jesus Christ, you come from above and tell us about heavenly things — things you know about firsthand, and things beyond our comprehension.

You come from another world, beyond time, and certify that God is with us.

You come and give of your Spirit without measure, although we do not know how to measure it within us.

You tell us of your Father's love for you, and for us, and how he has placed us into your careful hands, now and forever.

You call us to believe in you, because you are love.

You tell us that life is eternal for those who believe in you, and you tell us that eternal life has already begun.

Lord Jesus, if I know I love you out of fear of God's wrath, I do not love you. If it's the hope of eternal life that makes me love you, I do not love you truly. Even as you have no reason, beyond love, to love me, so must I love. All other motives are wicked.

"Wicked." What an awful word to use in prayer to you! You started this going, Lord, not me! You loved first, and that loving needed my heart. Now my heart needs you. Unless we are together, I am bereft of purpose. I am altogether lonely and alone. I am most miserable without you.

You, Lord, are the groom. With John the Baptist, I am your beloved, and I happily await the fullness of your coming, our wedding day. Amen.

15. THE WILL TO LISTEN

John 4:1-42

Now when Jesus learned that the Pharisees had heard, "Jesus is making and baptizing more disciples than John" — although it was not Jesus himself but his disciples who baptized — he left Judea and started back to Galilee. But he had to go through Samaria. So he came to a Samaritan city called Sychar, near the plot of ground that Jacob had given to his son Joseph. Jacob's well was there, and Jesus, tired out by his journey, was sitting by the well. It was about noon.

A Samaritan woman came to draw water, and Jesus said to her, "Give me a drink." (His disciples had gone to the city to buy food.) The Samaritan woman said to him, "How is it that you, a Jew, ask a drink of me, a woman of Samaria?" (Jews do not share things in common with Samaritans.) Jesus answered her, "If you knew the gift of God, and who it is that is saying to you, 'Give me a drink,' you would have asked him, and he would have given you living water." The woman said to him, "Sir, you have no bucket, and the well is deep. Where do you get that living water? Are you greater than our ancestor Jacob, who gave us the well, and with his sons and his flocks drank from it?" Jesus said to her, "Everyone who drinks of this water will be thirsty again, but those who drink of the water that I will give them will never be thirsty. The water that I will give will become in them a spring of water gushing up to eternal life." The woman said to him, "Sir, give me this water, so that I may never be thirsty or have to keep coming here to draw water."

Jesus said to her, "Go, call your husband, and come back." The woman answered him, "I have no husband." Jesus said to her, "You are right in saying, 'I have no husband,' for you have had five husbands, and the one you have now is not your husband. What you have said is true!" The woman said to him, "Sir, I see that you are a prophet. Our ancestors worshiped on this mountain, but you say that the place where people must worship is in Jerusalem." Jesus said to her, "Woman, believe me, the hour is coming when you will worship the Father neither on this mountain nor in Jerusalem. You worship what you do not know; we worship what we know, for salvation is from the Jews. But the hour is coming, and is now here, when the true worshipers will worship the Father in spirit and truth, for the Father seeks such as these to worship him. God is spirit, and those who worship him must worship in spirit and truth." The woman said to him, "I know that Messiah is coming (who is called Christ). When he comes, he will proclaim all things to us." Jesus said to her, "I am he, the one who is speaking to you."

Just then his disciples came. They were astonished that he was speaking with a woman, but no one said, "What do you want?" or, "Why are you speaking with her?" Then the woman left her water jar and went back to the city. She said to the people, "Come and see a man who told me everything I have ever done! He cannot be the Messiah, can he?" They left the city and were on their way to him.

Meanwhile the disciples were urging him, "Rabbi, eat something." But he said to them, "I have food to eat that you do not know about." So the disciples said to one another, "Surely no one has brought him something to eat?" Jesus said to them, "My food is to do the will of him who sent me and to complete his work. Do you not say, 'Four months more, then comes the harvest'? But I tell you, look around you, and see how the fields are ripe for harvesting. The reaper is already receiving wages and is gathering fruit for eternal life, so that sower and reaper may rejoice together. For here the saying holds true, 'One sows and another reaps.' I sent you to reap that for which you did not labor. Others have labored, and you have entered into their labor."

Many Samaritans from that city believed in him because of the woman's testimony, "He told me everything I have ever done." So when the Samaritans came to him, they asked him to stay with them; and he stayed there two days. And many more believed because of his word. They said to the woman, "It is no longer because of what you said that we believe, for we have heard for ourselves, and we know that this is truly the Savior of the world."

COMMENTARY

From a deep theological discussion, immediately preceding this episode, to a chance meeting at a well in Samaria, Jesus teaches. The profound and the mundane are equal arenas for his presence.

Jesus is neither anti-intellectual nor pro-illiterate. He simply doesn't make the arena narrow. Wherever we are in life, there he wants to meet us, on our turf, at our jobs, with our individual histories.

Jesus knows what he has been called to, which is to do the will of him who sent him. As Kierkegaard rightly proclaimed centuries later, "Purity of heart is to will one thing." That one thing is to be God's person, always.

PRAYER 15

Lord, it is demeaning to the committed that you let a Samaritan woman of bad reputation hear your first admission to being the Messiah. Surely there were people who dedicated their lives to the spiritual who yearned to hear you say it. Surely, Nicodemus would have been open to it, or almost any of your disciples. Such revelations to riffraff make us wonder, forever, if all our prayers and searchings matter one iota to you. It makes us wonder if we wouldn't be better off hauling water than studying your word.

Yes, I know that you get around to us who think about you day and night. Yes, I appreciate the challenge you give us to interpret, and study, and trust you to show up in due time; but no, I don't appreciate the years of dusty silence when faith alone is all there is to keep hope alive. I don't appreciate what feels like near neglect from one whose name is love.

It wasn't a very deep faith she had, was it? She was impressed, of course, with your knowledge of her life, as any of us would be. She used that same impression to make the others curious about your ability. Yet those others, like me, finally concluded that her witness wasn't enough. They needed some time with you alone.

Lord, she did ask some pretty good questions after you impressed her. She did perceive that you were at least a prophet. She did know about the coming of the Messiah. She did believe the Messiah would reveal all. You hooked her with your insight, and then you filled her with spiritual drink. You picked out one who wouldn't run off crying, "Blasphemy, blasphemy!" when you announced your identity. You simply gave her more to think about than she or we could handle.

Lord, make me as willing to listen as this woman was. Give me ears to hear you in the everyday events of my life. Give me eyes to see you at my daily chores. Give me the wisdom of those who heard the witness, to find some time to be with you alone, so that I may believe for myself. Amen.

16. DOING LOVE

John 4:43-54

When the two days were over, he went from that place to Galilee (for Jesus himself had testified that a prophet has no honor in the prophet's own country). When he came to Galilee, the Galileans welcomed him, since they had seen all that he had done in Jerusalem at the festival; for they all had gone to the festival.

Then he came again to Cana in Galilee where he had changed the water into wine. Now there was a royal official whose son lay ill in Capernaum. When he heard that Jesus had come from Judea to Galilee, he went and begged him to come down and heal his son, for he was at the point of death. Then Jesus said to him, "Unless you see signs and wonders you will not believe." The official said to him, "Sir, come down before my little boy dies." Jesus said to him, "Go, your son will live." The man believed the word that Jesus spoke to him and started on his way. As he was going down, his slaves met him and told him that his child was alive. So he asked them the hour when he began to recover, and they said to him, "Yesterday, at one in the afternoon the fever left him." The father realized that this was the hour when Jesus had said to him, "Your son will live." So he himself believed, along with his whole household. Now this was the second sign that Jesus did after coming from Judea to Galilee.

COMMENTARY

Jesus seems to be suspicious of the motives of those coming to him, for many had seen all that he had done at the festival. So, when a royal officer is willing to risk his reputation by asking Jesus for help, Jesus wonders aloud about the integrity of the motives.

Jesus' defensiveness is expressed by his theological concern, "Unless you see signs and wonders you will not believe," whereas the officer disarms this suspicion by a father's love, "Sir, come down before my little boy dies."

The simplicity of the father's need and the clarity of his faith wins Jesus' response, and both the boy and the father derive the benefit.

PRAYER 16

It's usually the other way around, Lord. I want to speak theology, while you want to do love. Thank you for healing the boy through a father's faith. Thank you for hearing his simple heartfelt plea.

I must wonder if the child would have died without his father's trip to you? And I wonder if the father had answered wrongly, what the consequences of his mistake would have been? Would you have given the boy life if the father had been faithless?

As you can see, Lord, I still prefer questions to actions, analysis over facts, and complexity over simplicity. How will you ever get me to take a story at its face value, and simply let love be? Why must I argue with you over everything? Am I really afraid of letting you do something significant without my feeble approval that says, "Yes, that fits my idea of an appropriate response from you"?

Lord, when I try to live simply, trust blindly, and not ask questions, I feel like I'm being naive, or even lazy in the faith. I feel as though I'm skipping through important insights into your nature. I feel as though I might be missing the point.

Help me ask the right questions, Lord, and not the same ones over and over that you have either repeatedly answered, or I cannot comprehend. Let me learn how to be content with your silence on certain matters, and to answer your questions to me as simply as this loving father did. Remind me to bring before you those I love who need your healing touch, and when you grant the return of health, remind me to give you the thanks.

Thank you, Lord, for healing this father's son. Thank you. Amen.

17. SAYING "YES" TO HEALING

John 5:1-18

After this there was a festival of the Jews, and Jesus went up to Jerusalem.

Now in Jerusalem by the Sheep Gate there is a pool, called in Hebrew Bethzatha, which has five porticoes. In these lay many invalids — blind, lame, and paralyzed. One man was there who had been ill for thirty-eight years. When Jesus saw him lying there and knew that he had been there a long time, he said to him, "Do you want to be made well?" The sick man answered him, "Sir, I have no one to put me into the pool when the water is stirred up; and while I am making my way, someone else steps down ahead of me." Jesus said to him, "Stand up, take your mat and walk." At once the man was made well, and he took up his mat and began to walk.

Now that day was a sabbath. So the Jews said to the man who had been cured, "It is the sabbath; it is not lawful for you to carry your mat." But he answered them, "The man who made me well said to me, 'Take up your mat and walk.'" They asked him, "Who is the man who said to you, 'Take it up and walk'?" Now the man who had been healed did not know who it was, for Jesus had disappeared in the crowd that was there. Later Jesus found him in the temple and said to him. "See, you have been made well! Do not sin any more, so that nothing worse happens to you." The man went away and told the Jews that it was Jesus who had made him well. Therefore the Jews started persecuting Jesus, because he was doing such things on the sabbath. But Jesus answered them, "My Father is still working, and I also am working." For this reason the Jews were seeking all the more to kill him, because he was not only breaking the sabbath, but was also calling God his own Father, thereby making himself equal to God.

COMMENTARY

The logic of staying thirty-eight years by a pool, knowing that one does not even have the strength to enter it for cure when the waters are stirred, pushes our credulity. Yet, it is easy to suppose that the persons gathered at the pool knew each other well, and the gathering of the afflicted was doubtlessly also a gathering for support and friendship. So, Jesus' question, "Do you want to be healed?" is no silly query, but one that affects this man's way of living forever.

The miracle was performed without the man's knowing who Jesus was. Two points are immediately clear: Jesus does not need our faith in order to exercise his power, and many of the miracles we receive are not properly credited to him.

The religious elite only found out about the healing because they saw the man carrying his mat in violation of the sabbath day's observance. When they began to persecute Jesus because of his threat to religious order, they quickly uncovered a bigger problem. Jesus defended his healing by aligning himself with the Father, who, as God, works every day to heal and sustain life on earth. This close identification with God the Father's sabbath work made his equality with God clear.

PRAYER 17

Lord, for many years I, and many others like me, have camped near the source of healing, but have not had the strength of character to move from our mats of misery. If you do not come by unexpectedly, what chance is there for a cure? Even if strength were sufficient to move toward you, unless you intervene, no cure can come.

Lord, what is there about our mats that we like so much? Are we guilty of enjoying ill health for a lifetime? Are we that lost? Are we that afraid of moving into a new future with you as Lord? Do we know that you look for us in the temple, that you give thanks to the Father when we recognize our cure came from you?

Our questions betray our fears, and we know that we are not yet ready to let you have our whole life, our whole will, our whole self. Like the Israelites wandering in the wilderness, we are afraid we would look back at our bondage as "not so bad" compared to the uncertainty of being your person, your example of power waged, of healing completed. What can we say to those who ask us, "Who brought this change upon you?" Do we have to name your name, and so be marked as one of yours?

This is, of course, what happened to you, except you were not the object of cure, but the healer. Even you had to give account. You were put on the spot for doing good, and when you answered, you didn't answer in a way that fit the theology of the day. The quick minds nailed you early. They knew what your answer implied. They saw you and the Father as one. They knew that such unity of will was not possible among mortals. They knew what you were implying. They knew. You knew. We know.

Lord Jesus Christ, what would it mean to my life to be united with your life? Could you give me a glimpse of what that would look like? I don't see much glory to it, at least not now. I don't see much peace of mind. I see crosses and ridicule, uncertainty and danger. I see new temptations coming, the size of which I could not handle. I see living with less. I see open rebellion to the ways of this world. I see too much suffering, Lord, to do it. I see you asking for more than I can give.

Lord, could you just nudge me off my mat a little?

Oh, Lord, how unsettled I am because of you, how fidgety, how fitful. I am not at peace with my way, and I am quite afraid of your way. Is there no middle course? Can I not wait a little longer? Is it today you come by my mat, after all these many years of waiting, to ask, "Are you ready? Do you want me to heal you? Do you want to be baptized in the Spirit?"

Help me say yes, Lord, help me say yes, else I will never be your person. Show me again what the future looks like side by side with you. Give me a picture of your constant presence. Fill me with your promise to walk with me always. Keep talking to me Lord, keep talking, until I rise from my mat and walk, saying, "Yes, yes, yes." Amen.

18. JUDGMENT

John 5:19-30

Jesus said to them, "Very truly, I tell you, the Son can do nothing on his own, but only what he sees the Father doing; for whatever the Father does, the Son does likewise. The Father loves the Son and shows him all that he himself is doing; and he will show him greater works than these, so that you will be astonished. Indeed, just as the Father raises the dead and gives them life, so also the Son gives life to whomever he wishes. The Father judges no one but has given all judgment to the Son, so that all may honor the Son just as they honor the Father. Anyone who does not honor the Son does not honor the Father who sent him. Very truly, I tell you, anyone who hears my word and believes him who sent me has eternal life, and does not come under judgment, but has passed from death to life.

"Very truly, I tell you, the hour is coming, and is now here, when the dead will hear the voice of the Son of God, and those who hear will live. For just as the Father has life in himself, so he has granted the Son also to have life in himself, and he has given him authority to execute judgment, because he is the Son of Man. Do not be astonished at this; for the hour is coming when all who are in their graves will hear his voice and will come out — those who have done good, to the resurrection of life, and those who have done evil, to the resurrection of condemnation.

"I can do nothing on my own. As I hear, I judge; and my judgment is just, because I seek to do not my own will but the will of him who sent me."

COMMENTARY

The alliance and attachment between the Father and the Son is portrayed in functional terms, but that relationship is based solely on the love that the Father and the Son have for each other. In a simple factual manner, Jesus states the truth, "The Father loves the Son."

From this reality, all sorts of godly uncommon work occurs on our behalf. Jesus is empowered to do works to astonish us, to raise up the dead, to have life in himself, and to be our judge. There is an hour coming when all who are in their graves will hear the voice of the Son, and the dead will have no choice but to face the Christ as judge.

PRAYER 18

Lord Jesus Christ, it is far more comforting to think of you as our judge than it is to think of your Father as our judge. You have been here, like us, and you know how easy it is to go astray. You know all about the limitations placed upon us as people, simply because we have bodies, finite minds, lots of responsibility, busy lives, and tricky situations to figure out.

We are glad you are to be our judge, rather than your Father, even if we are to pray, "Our Father." Earthly fathers don't have the best reputation for being understanding and compassionate. Some of us know this from personal experience.

Lord Jesus Christ, sometimes we like to think of you as a soft-touch, a pushover, easier on us than some crusty old judge who pores over volumes of musty old books to find out a new way to penalize the guilty. We like to think of you saying, "That's okay. I understand. You did your best, and that's all I wanted you to do." We like to imagine you saying, "I'm going to save everybody anyway, so 'be happy, don't worry.'"

Yet, Lord, we have more than a nagging suspicion that these thoughts do not come from you, but from our enemy, who would downplay the importance of our earthly existence, take away the purpose of our struggle, make us forget the awful war that wages in heaven, and so blur right and wrong as to make judgment unnecessary after all.

> No judgment?
> What a relief that would be!?
> > (No, it wouldn't.)
> What freedom!?
> > (Not really.)
> No more fear of hell!?
> > (No more yearning for heaven.)

Lord, you are to be the judge, not a nonjudge. You are to tell us, one day, all that we did, and that thought fills us with a dread so deep that we cannot let the thought stay within our minds but for a moment. We know, intuitively, that we cannot stand before you on that day with anything but shame. We know that if we must say we're sorry, we will do so penitently, but we do not want to know what evil we have done to others; we do not want to know how our failures blocked others from you; we do not want to know everything we ever did that was wrong. We do not want to be judged by you, or by anyone. We just want to be forgiven.

Lord, we know we cannot earn our salvation. We know that we need you as our Savior. We know that the mountain of our sin is higher than the hill of our goodness. We know that we have no goodness at all, except what you have given us. Yet, knowing all this, we still dread that day of uncovering, that day of exposure, that day of nothing but sin to see. If you do not cover us up on that day, we shall surely be in hell.

Now that we have made these confessions to you, Lord Jesus, we hold on to the promise you made to all when you said, "I will be with you always." Be with us on our day of judgment. Love us as the Father loves you. And through your love, show us how wonderful the Father's love is after all, that we may thank him for you. Amen.

19. PRETENDING TO WANT GOD

John 5:31-47

"If I testify about myself, my testimony is not true. There is another who testifies on my behalf, and I know that his testimony to me is true. You sent messengers to John, and he testified to the truth. Not that I accept such human testimony, but I say these things so that you may be saved. He was a burning and shining lamp, and you were willing to rejoice for a while in his light. But I have a testimony greater than John's. The works that the Father has given me to complete, the very works that I am doing, testify on my behalf that the Father has sent me. And the Father who sent me has himself testified on my behalf. You have never heard his voice or seen his form, and you do not have his word abiding in you, because you do not believe him whom he has sent.

"You search the scriptures because you think that in them you have eternal life; and it is they that testify on my behalf. Yet you refuse to come to me to have life. I do not accept glory from human beings. But I know that you do not have the love of God in you. I have come in my Father's name, and you do not accept me; if another comes in his own name, you will accept him. How can you believe when you accept glory from one another and do not seek the glory that comes from the one who alone is God? Do not think that I accuse you before the Father; your accuser is Moses, on whom you have set your hope. If you believed Moses, you would believe me, for he wrote about me. But if you do not believe what he wrote, how will you believe what I say?"

COMMENTARY

Trying to weigh the evidence about Jesus is a little like trying to figure out if someone loves you by adding up "the score." Jesus reminds those who sought to discredit him that John the Baptist testified on his behalf. He points very profoundly at the Father who is giving him power to perform miracles. He even senses their fear of judgment by him, but tells them it's Moses they ought to fear, since he's the one they're trying to follow, but cannot.

The distinctions between the way of God in Christ and the way of religion in general are being sharply drawn. On the one hand there is gospel and assigned work from the Father; on the other there is the law of Moses. On the one hand there is the glory of God; on the other, the glory of whatever a recent human leader's charisma can inspire. One set of evidence is from God, the other is based solely upon ever-changing human rationale or emotion.

The passage ends with a question regarding the *how* of belief. How are we ever to come to faith, if it is based on persons or systems doomed to failure? Jesus is lifting our hopes higher, much higher, so that our hope is in the Father who sent him. Jesus is pointing again, and, as always, he is pointing at the Heavenly Father.

PRAYER 19

Lord Jesus, arguing your case with nonbelievers is futile, and we must only suppose you do it for believers to listen in on the conversation. You know better than any of us that we will not come to faith through intellectual persuasion, for if we did, we would have something less than faith. You know that we can search the Scripture forever and not find faith, or God, or you, unless the Holy Spirit opens our hearts.

This is both a comfort to us and an escape. If you don't open up our hearts, we can relax and say, "I tried," or we can even blame it on your weak Spirit not doing the job! You put us in what feels like a win-win situation, by making it impossible to come to faith without your Father's permission, and then letting us fault you, or the Father, or the Spirit, when faith is absent. Why would you do this to yourself? How can you judge us, ultimately, if we take a few hesitant steps in your direction, but find nothing in front of us but void and darkness? Don't you see how we think about these matters? Don't you understand that we would rather blame God for our nonbelief than ourselves? Don't you see how clever we are in our rational minds?

Lord, we know that these arguments are without integrity. We know something crucial is missing. We know that such "searching" for you is not searching for you at all, but searching for a way to escape from you with our wills and intellects and our own life goals totally intact. We know that you can see through all of our phony attempts to pretend to want you in our lives, without really wanting you in our lives. And if we can discern these things, how much more are you able to see through our lame excuses?

Lord, you are a pearl of great price that must be sought with our whole being. You are a treasure in a field that requires the selling of all that we are in order to embrace the wealth that you are. You are infinite in Spirit, boundless in riches, endless in being. Going after you is the adventure of our lives, and we too often make it into work rather than joy.

Lord, give to us the joy of pursuit. May we search you out like a lost hiker looks for a companion friend in the forest ... a friend who knows the only way out, a friend who is not lost. Give us the joy of pursuit, like friends looking for friends who are dreadfully missed, like a lover looking for the beloved.

Sustain our search with the good news that you are not in hiding at all, but have been dropping giant hints of your whereabouts in every moment of our day, in every event of our lives. Sustain us with the truth that you are in search of us, looking for ways to break into our crusty hearts. Surprise us with your presence, and when we take note that you are there, give us the presence of mind to say thank you, and the impulse to smile. Amen.

20. RUNNING TO THE MOUNTAIN

John 6:1-15

After this Jesus went to the other side of the Sea of Galilee, also called the Sea of Tiberias. A large crowd kept following him, because they saw the signs that he was doing for the sick. Jesus went up the mountain and sat down there with his disciples. Now the Passover, the festival of the Jews, was near. When he looked up and saw a large crowd coming toward him, Jesus said to Philip, "Where are we to buy bread for these people to eat?" He said this to test him, for he himself knew what he was going to do. Philip answered him, "Six months' wages would not buy enough bread for each of them to get a little." One of his disciples, Andrew, Simon Peter's brother, said to him, "There is a boy here who has five barley loaves and two fish. But what are they among so many people?" Jesus said, "Make the people sit down." Now there was a great deal of grass in the place; so they sat down, about five thousand in all. Then Jesus took the loaves, and when he had given thanks, he distributed them to those who were seated; so also the fish, as much as they wanted. When they were satisfied, he told his disciples, "Gather up the fragments left over, so that nothing may be lost." So they gathered them up, and from the fragments of the five barley loaves, left by those who had eaten, they filled twelve baskets. When the people saw the sign that he had done, they began to say, "This is indeed the prophet who is to come into the world."

When Jesus realized that they were about to come and take him by force to make him king, he withdrew again to the mountain by himself.

COMMENTARY

This is the only miracle found in every one of the four Gospels. John is clearly trying to show how the people followed Jesus because of the signs he did, mostly in the healing of the sick. That he could also feed the hungry was no little bonus. The implications of not having to produce food anymore are staggering.

As Jesus became candidate number one to be king, his response was to go off by himself "to the mountain." It was time to pray things over.

PRAYER 20

Jesus, you ran for cover again. This is not the first time you found yourself too popular for your own good ... too popular for our good. Was it for yourself that you ran to the mountain to pray, or for us?

Lord, we've trained ourselves to take advantage of every opportunity, to call it a "call" when people want us to step forward in your church and lead. We yearn for the moment when that call is extended, and trust that your Holy Spirit has been at work. We spend our lives trying to be faithful to you by indicating our willingness to do even more, but here you are, the "caller," in retreat to the mountain.

Why did you go there, Lord? Was it simply to get away from the people who would make you king after you fed them in the wilderness? Was the kingship a temptation for you, or simply a sign that we, the people, were missing the point of your presence again?

What did you do when you got there, Lord — what did you say? Were you elated or dejected? Did you ask the Father what to do, or did you just go there by yourself to plan your next move?

Lord, you have shown that you have power over illness, and power to produce. Everything is under your rule. You are far beyond a kingship of this world. Yet we seek to make you such a king, just as Satan did — a king of this world's stuff. We are still worried about very practical matters, like health, food, natural disasters, and evil rule. We have no mountain, like you, to retreat to when things get confusing.

Lord, are we at that mountain now, even as these thoughts pass through our hearts and minds? Are we doing what you did when you went to your mountain? Are we being faithful by asking questions of you, endless questions, or do you just want us to come into your presence for joy? We can hardly do it, without asking.

Here we are, Lord, alone with you, listening intently to your Spirit, ready to become what you are.

You say, "No need to become, you already are."

You say, "No need to do greater things, just lesser things."

You say, "No need to become a king. Better to be my child."

You say, "No need to force out of life what is given freely by me."

You say, "Love is not as hard a task as you are making it."

You say, "I am not a spark of divine within you, struggling for notice, but I stand before you, always asking you to let me in."

Lord, this day, be our noticeable guide. Let all that comes into our lives be opportunity for you. As we walk, walk with us, and as we talk, talk for us. As we think, remind us of your nearness. And as we reflect, may we see you with us. Amen.

21. STORMS AND CALM

John 6:16-21
When evening came, his disciples went down to the sea, got into a boat, and started across the sea to Capernaum. It was now dark, and Jesus had not yet come to them. The sea became rough because a strong wind was blowing. When they had rowed about three or four miles, they saw Jesus walking on the sea and coming near the boat, and they were terrified. But he said to them, "It is I; do not be afraid." Then they wanted to take him into the boat, and immediately the boat reached the land toward which they were going.

COMMENTARY

By now it must have been obvious to the disciples that Jesus was going to absent himself from them frequently. But it was not so much to get away from them as it was to be in touch with the Father. The solitude of prayer precedes the walk on the stormy sea.

PRAYER 21

Lord Jesus Christ, it is easy to imagine the fear that a dark stormy sea at night produced in your disciples, especially at a time when boats didn't have engines to help them meet the waves. But it doesn't seem to be the darkness, the wind, the waves, nor the deep that frightened your chosen. You did.

Lord, if you come into my life during a storm, as real as you came into the lives of your disciples, again you will have to identify yourself and tell me not to be afraid. Who can stand the sight of you, even under the most perfect circumstances? How can I dare ask you to be so present that even the storm of my life dissipates by your nearness? Lord, I am afraid to have you that close, afraid that I would mistake you for some other dread, afraid that I would not take my eye off my storm to see your calm.

Jesus, I have asked you, sincerely, to come into my life. I have asked you to come and be present, to use me, to give me direction, but almost always, when I sense you near, you bring as much storm as you do calm. In fact, you always seem to reverse my state: if I am in a storm, you bring calm; if I am calm, you bring a storm. What does this mean?

Sometimes, Lord, I have been sorry that I've invited you in, because you are not always such pleasant company. You literally answer my prayer, but in ways I don't like. Yes, I want to be used, but used nicely. Yes, I want to be your witness, but in safe ways. Yes, I want to be very bold and very brave, but I don't want to be formed by suffering. I just want you to do all the work, keep me from making mistakes or enemies, let me be a good example of your love, and enjoy this good life that you, yourself, have made possible with the Father.

How silly I am, Lord, to think that you can use me without using me. I know what you do with those you choose. It is not a pretty picture, which is why, I think, I don't really volunteer to be your person. I'm too afraid for that. I did it when I was young, before I knew your ways. Now I know you too well. I know what you do. Not only am I afraid of the pain, but I am also afraid that I will fail you in the end. I am afraid that I will be another Judas, not another Paul. Yet, you already have your hooks in deep ... deep, beyond the barb. To walk away from you now is to rip out my very heart. I am afraid to go, afraid to stay, afraid that you will come to me in my storm, afraid that you will not. What kind of God are you to make me so fearful?

Lord, you spoke two quick messages to your storm-tossed disciples. It was all that they could bear to hear, all that they needed to hear. You told them you were there. You told them not to be afraid. And then you brought a peace; then you brought them to the place where they were heading. Nothing dangerous could make you sink away. Nothing slippery could make you fall. No darkness could cover you up. You were master of the storm, master of the sea, but most importantly, master of the frightened ones.

Lord, like the disciples, I may not have enough sense to ask for you to come at the right moment in the storms of my life, but you will be there. You will show up. And if you do not show up as quickly as I think you should, and if I do not recognize you, even when you're there, do for me what you did for them, and bring me safely to the destination of my life; bring me safely to you. Amen.

22. LOVE HUNGER

John 6:22-34

The next day the crowd that had stayed on the other side of the sea saw that there had been only one boat there. They also saw that Jesus had not got into the boat with his disciples, but that his disciples had gone away alone. Then some boats from Tiberias came near the place where they had eaten the bread after the Lord had given thanks. So when the crowd saw that neither Jesus nor his disciples were there, they themselves got into the boats and went to Capernaum looking for Jesus.

When they found him on the other side of the sea, they said to him, "Rabbi, when did you come here?" Jesus answered them, "Very truly, I tell you, you are looking for me, not because you saw signs, but because you ate your fill of the loaves. Do not work for the food that perishes, but for the food that endures for eternal life, which the Son of Man will give you. For it is on him that God the Father has set his seal." Then they said to him, "What must we do to perform the works of God?" Jesus answered them, "This is the work of God, that you believe in him whom he has sent." So they said to him, "What sign are you going to give us then, so that we may see it and believe you? What work are you performing? Our ancestors ate the manna in the wilderness; as it is written, 'He gave them bread from heaven to eat.'" Then Jesus said to them, "Very truly, I tell you, it was not Moses who gave you the bread from heaven, but it was my Father who gives you the true bread from heaven. For the bread of God is that which comes down from heaven and gives life to the world." They said to him, "Sir, give us this bread always."

COMMENTARY

This passage is filled with phrases that reveal important details about the workings of Christ. For example, the feeding of the multitude was identified neither by the huge number of people who were fed nor by the place where it occurred. It was simply the meal they had eaten "after the Lord had given thanks." The giving of thanks by the Lord was more important than the other details.

Also, their "looking for Jesus" parallels most of our "looking for Jesus." It is a simple search to view the person of Jesus; but watch out when we find him! He is not some oddity to be seen from a distance, but more like a dangerous bear to be encountered. If we only want to look at him from a distance, we can be safe. Once we talk with him, however, it is not safe, even to watch. It is not safe, even to ask, "Where have you been?"

Finally, all that we've settled in our minds as the way God works is subject to radical disruption, if we talk with Christ. Note the conversation in John. He won't let us use our theology on him. He won't let us interpret what God did years ago, but he will tell us what really happened then, and what is expected now. He is not a history lesson to be learned, but a rendezvous with the living Holy Spirit.

PRAYER 22

Lord, it takes some courage even to open up a conversation with you, if you're going to make it into something other than a polite "Good morning." Maybe that's why we like to do all the talking. You're safer that way.

Your giving thanks before the breaking of bread impressed the people. Surely it wasn't that unusual. Surely you did it regularly. It must have been something you said, something you did during the prayer that drew the attention. Maybe you asked the Father to multiply the loaves. Maybe you upbraided the crowd for its stinginess. Maybe you looked different when you prayed. We don't know, but something seems to have happened that isn't recorded, else the event would not have been associated with that prayer.

Lord, like the crowd, we look for you nearly every day. We look to see if we can see you around. We like to know you are near. Just the sight of you, your general words of advice, your ability to do whatever you want to do, impresses us. It impressed them, too. You are a very good show at times.

So we are not that surprised with what you did to their opening remark. We are not surprised you took them to task. You don't want to be the object of curiosity seekers, any more than the rest of us. You just won't be watched for entertainment's sake, without causing some discomfort to the spectator. It wasn't exactly guilt you inflicted, but it was a scolding, followed by a command. You nailed their selfish motive up for all to see and then gave a better reason to look for you. Through you the Heavenly Father has sent a better food than loaf bread.

Lord, they sensed you spoke truly. They began to sense their hunger for something other than free bread. They began to see that you were more than a ticket to a food line. You were the food.

You talk about eternal life as though it's something that needs to be begun now, not later. You talk about food that is given, not earned. You talk about having the Father's seal of approval upon yourself, like some sort of consumer protection and endorsement. You point to the Father and to yourself at one and the same moment, as though you are in this thing together, as though to know one of you is to know the other. And because you tell us what's going on between you and the Father, you include us all in this thing together.

Lord, what is this "thing" we are in together? What is happening to us because of you and the Father? Do you still have some cosmic battle going on with Satan, and, like Job, we cannot know about it? Lord, how do we fight with you, if we do not even know why? Are we the prize?

No other reason makes sense. Surely you can snuff out Satan like a candle, if you want to. It can't be Satan alone. You can take away our doubt in an instant, if you want to. It can't be our weakness alone. You can turn us into anything else you want us to be, without so much as a memory on our part of what you had intended for us from the beginning. It can't be simply because we're human. Yet, Lord, there is something about even your power. It's as though you can't have us unless we want you above all else. It's as though you are powerless to convince us of your love, except by your love. It's as though you have given the enemy 10,000 weapons to win us, and yourself only one.

Lord Jesus Christ, we will never figure it all out, but you, alone, are beautiful. You, alone, are the way. Help us ward off temptations too tempting to ignore. Help us keep our eye on you, the bread that nourishes for a life yet to come. And, when we are there together in the next life, remind us of these days of worry when we wondered too much about your wisdom. It will make us smile. Amen.

23. ETERNAL BREAD

John 6:35-40

Jesus said to them, "I am the bread of life. Whoever comes to me will never be hungry, and whoever believes in me will never be thirsty. But I said to you that you have seen me and yet do not believe. Everything that the Father gives me will come to me, and anyone who comes to me I will never drive away; for I have come down from heaven, not to do my own will, but the will of him who sent me. And this is the will of him who sent me, that I should lose nothing of all that he has given me, but raise it up on the last day. This is indeed the will of my Father, that all who see the Son and believe in him may have eternal life; and I will raise them up on the last day."

COMMENTARY

The intense partnership between Christ and the Father is outlined in this passage. The Father's mandate to Jesus is stated, as well as Jesus' devotion to it.

Nine times the word "will" is used in the short passage above, five times in reference to the future, and four times in reference to the desires of God the Father. What God wants, and what's going to be, is clear. Nothing can stop the future that is coming, nor the intent of God.

PRAYER 23

Lord, to "lose nothing at all," as the Father willed for you (for our sakes), is more than anyone could hope for, and more than any one of us has experienced. In fact, it seems as though our losses are constantly increasing. We lose our health, our loved ones, our peace of mind, our purpose. We lose our vigor, our courage, our confidence in our own usefulness, yet you say that nothing, no one, will be lost to you.

Lord, we know your history. We know what you lost. You lost everything in the end. You lost Judas as a disciple. You lost your case before Pilate. You lost all but one of your disciples while on the cross. You lost, or "gave away," Mary, your mother, to John.

You lost, or perhaps you "gave away," your very will, not only in Gethsemane, but also on Golgotha — especially on Golgotha. For at least a moment, maybe longer, you lost feeling the nearness of our Father. The spear opened up your side and the blood and water of your earthly body were lost to the ground. Though you could have had angels come to the rescue, you lost your life. You breathed a final breath. You lost, Lord Jesus Christ, you lost. You lost big.

And before any of this happens you say that you are the bread of life. You say that you can be consumed and eaten, like daily bread. You say that your losing way is life indeed, and that you are destined to lose nothing at all.

Yes, Lord, we see all the "wills" that talk about the future in your words to the nonbelievers. We know you are talking about "later on." You have your eyes focused back into that realm where we can only travel by imagination. You remember from where you came. You know that the place is real, that the Father is loving, and that time and troubles and losses in this life are not to be compared with coming joy. You make us have to lose our trust in our own experience.

How are we to give up these good senses of sight and smell and taste and touch? How are we to go against the very gifts given us for survival? Are we not to use our own heads, our own eyes and ears, to protect us from danger?

Yes, Lord, "survival" is a relative term. Yes, clearly there is no survival possible on the earth. The generations rise and fall on schedule. None of us lasts very long. So, you make your point. "After the last breath," you ask, "then what? After the final loss, what is there, if not me?"

Lord, help me recognize the taste of eternal bread, your body. Help me see that when you physically enter my body, Satan himself, with all his poison, cannot kill me forever. Feed me, gentle Jesus, with your Spirit, so that my "losses" are recognized only as gains, as baggage shed, ideas corrected, failures forgiven, and loved ones committed into your eternal care. Amen.

24. LOVE POWER

John 6:41-59

Then the Jews began to complain about him because he said, "I am the bread that came down from heaven." They were saying, "Is not this Jesus, the son of Joseph, whose father and mother we know? How can he now say, 'I have come down from heaven'?" Jesus answered them, "Do not complain among yourselves. No one can come to me unless drawn by the Father who sent me; and I will raise that person up on the last day. It is written in the prophets, 'And they shall all be taught by God.' Everyone who has heard and learned from the Father comes to me. Not that anyone has seen the Father except the one who is from God; he has seen the Father. Very truly, I tell you, whoever believes has eternal life. I am the bread of life. Your ancestors ate the manna in the wilderness, and they died. This is the bread that comes down from heaven, so that one may eat of it and not die. I am the living bread that came down from heaven. Whoever eats of this bread will live forever; and the bread that I will give for the life of the world is my flesh."

The Jews then disputed among themselves, saying, "How can this man give us his flesh to eat?" So Jesus said to them, "Very truly, I tell you, unless you eat the flesh of the Son of Man and drink his blood, you have no life in you. Those who eat my flesh and drink my blood have eternal life, and I will raise them up on the last day; for my flesh is true food and my blood is true drink. Those who eat my flesh and drink my blood abide in me, and I in them. Just as the living Father sent me, and I live because of the Father, so whoever eats me will live because of me. This is the bread that came down from heaven, not like that which your ancestors ate, and they died. But the one who eats this bread will live forever." He said these things while he was teaching in the synagogue at Capernaum.

COMMENTARY

The dispute that Jesus' listeners got themselves embroiled in with one another was a secondary point. They had practical questions about "how" a person could eat the flesh and drink the blood of another, while Jesus was teaching them that the Father draws people to faith, draws them to Christ, like a stream in a desert place draws life to itself.

The busy, active work of the Father is further illuminated by calling him "the living Father," as opposed, perhaps, to dead ancestral fathers. This is no father descended from others. This is the author of life, the originator, the sustainer of it all. This is not fatherhood as we normally understand it. This is creator God whose synonym is love.

The motivation of this love God has also revealed. It is for the "life of the world." In complete agreement with John 3:16, it is "the life of the world" that is the object of his love. Although it becomes intensely personal, when it is us he has targeted for his favor, the big surprise is that the draw we feel to love is a gift from the Father. It is evidence, primal evidence, of his individual work in each of us. Any impulse to love is evidence of his individual work in us. Without him, we would never do it ... we would never love, not another, ever.

PRAYER 24

Heavenly Father, you've done it to us. You've drawn us to love. Maybe we haven't loved very well or very often, but we've done it. We haven't always gotten all the love we've wanted from others, but what came, came from you. Thank you. We see love everywhere on special days. Hospitals filled with anxious loved ones sitting there, waiting for a miracle. We see it on the street, through recognition of another's humanity. We see it between persons, one looking into the window of the soul of another. Marvelous love. Infiltrating the world. Saving it from disaster. Love, the most awesome experience, the rarest event in the cosmos, the one thing void of selfishness, the one phenomenon that will be forever inexplicable, except it comes from you.

Lord Jesus Christ, you, alone, have seen the Father. You are his perfect reflection, the magnet that draws all lovers to God. You are the image we see when we think of God. All people who love will one day worship you, because you are love incarnate, love within us. You are not only the perfect example of love, but also love loving, even now. Who can resist you and have peace of mind? Who can refuse you and pretend you aren't near? Who can ever love or be loved, without it being you in the middle, you as the bread, you as the drink that makes it happen?

Your love is life, the only life that matters. Your love is the life of the world, the heartbeat, the pulse. Your love is no mere emotion or sentiment; it is the power to live without fear, with an expectant eye on doing so forever.

Heavenly Father, Lord Jesus Christ, your Spirit fills all life with love. Hear now the echo of your words, by what we say to others. See now the reflection of your work, by what we do. Feel now, the strength of your compassion as evidenced by ours. As we are fed by your Son, we taste eternal life. Come, now, abide with us, and we with you, forever. Amen.

25. BEYOND FLESH

John 6:60-71

When many of his disciples heard it, they said, "This teaching is difficult; who can accept it?" But Jesus, being aware that his disciples were complaining about it, said to them, "Does this offend you? Then what if you were to see the Son of Man ascending to where he was before? It is the spirit that gives life; the flesh is useless. The words that I have spoken to you are spirit and life. But among you there are some who do not believe." For Jesus knew from the first who were the ones that did not believe, and who was the one that would betray him. And he said, "For this reason, I have told you that no one can come to me unless it is granted by the Father."

Because of this many of his disciples turned back and no longer went about with him. So Jesus asked the twelve, "Do you also wish to go away?" Simon Peter answered him, "Lord, to whom can we go? You have the words of eternal life. We have come to believe and know that you are the Holy One of God." Jesus answered them, "Did I not choose you, the twelve? Yet one of you is a devil." He was speaking of Judas, son of Simon Iscariot, for he, though one of the twelve, was going to betray him.

COMMENTARY

"It is the spirit that gives life, the flesh is useless." True? Come now, would we have consciousness without a body? Would we know where we are, or who was with us, without a body? Are the words of "eternal life" more important than the way of earthly life? Our hearts may say "no," but our experience makes us wonder. Who are we, what are we, without a body? Who are we, what are we, if all we have are words, even if they be words of eternal life?

PRAYER 25

Lord Jesus Christ, who are you without the incarnation? Without your body, who are you? We cannot see you, touch you, hear you, except in a spiritual sense. That's why you came down, isn't it, to make yourself known on our terms? Now you tell us that the body is of no account. You tell us that it is the spirit that gives life, that the body is useless.

What are we to do with our infirmities, Lord? Ignore them? Should we pretend that our fleshly weaknesses do not matter? Shall we let the flesh die so that the spirit may reign?

"The flesh is useless." The message feels both true and false at the same time. Yes, the flesh is temporal, due to self-destruct shortly, yet without it, we are not here! The flesh is both beautiful and horrid in the same moment. Our dream is to live without the limitations of the physical, but it is the physical that shows us what you and the Father have created out of nothing. You made the physical, just as you made the spiritual. You said it was "good" — in fact, you said it was "very good."

Living with paradox, Lord, is like living as a schizophrenic. We are forever divided with allegiance. We do not know what side to take. Should we let this life go, entirely, and forget our physical needs (along, we suppose, with the physical needs of the poor?!), and should we just wallow in the spirit? We know we are not being fair. We know that we are not about to let go of our physical needs. We know that we are very much in the body and do not want out of it yet.

Lord, if the flesh is useless, why didn't you just bypass the physical universe when you made us? Instead of giving us bodies, why didn't you give us pure spirits instead? Why did you put us down here in a touchable, tangible, world? Why did you become flesh yourself? Why did you say that the flesh is useless? Is our whole purpose to find the way out of the physical world into the spiritual world? Are we supposed to look at our bodies as an obstacle to faith's development, or as the irrefutable anchor to the place where you want us to be for the time being?

Lord, this is the "time being." This moment, if there be such a thing, is as short as the whisker on an infant. If the *now* exists, if the moment has being, it is more fleeting than consciousness. What can we say except we know that the now is but an instant between the past and the future? How can we know you in terms of that short a time? If most everything is either past or future, what is the moment of this thought?

Lord, we would understand you. We would take away the mystery of life, and write it down in textbook style for all to read. We would explain the whys and wherefores as eloquently as the greatest orator, but you say "no" — not today, not now, not ever. You, Lord, are beyond time and space, beyond bodies and ideas, beyond questions and doubts. You let us live in bodies, in flesh, to prove that you inhabit all that is, yet you draw us away from bodies to spirit. You are forever pushing us out of what you put us in. You foil all logic to make us see that we cannot know you by deduction, cannot come to you through knowledge, cannot be convinced of your presence by reason.

Peter sensed it in your words. He sensed that you had "the words of eternal life," the same stuff with which you created the world by speaking. Peter knew, intuitively, that although he was in the body, the body was temporary. He knew there was more, that you were more, that words were more important than things.

Lord Jesus Christ, before the age of telecommunications, you believed your words would be recorded for all time, though you didn't know how.

Lord Jesus Christ, before you left your body on the cross for others to bury, you believed that you would be in paradise with a forgiven thief on the day of your dying.

Lord Jesus Christ, you talked with the Father, using only words. You believed your own message. You lived by the spirit.

Lord, come to us in memory, that we may recall your presence in our lives at the most surprising moments of our past. Come to us in the future. Come to us now with a message about the future. Come to us through imagination, for we can readily see you out there ahead of us, calling us forward. Come to us in this extended moment. Link many moments together so we can sing a whole song, pray a whole prayer. And, when you do extend the now, take away all questions and be with us for love's sake.

Lord Jesus Christ, where else can we go? You alone have the words of eternal life. No one else inspires us. Nothing else is true enough. No one else blends all our moments into holy presence, your presence. No one else, and no other thing, so totally swallows up every other way. You, alone, are the one holy alternative to despair. Amen.

26. BEYOND GENTLE LOVE

John 7:1-24

After this Jesus went about in Galilee. He did not wish to go about in Judea because the Jews were looking for an opportunity to kill him. Now the Jewish festival of Booths was near. So his brothers said to him, "Leave here and go to Judea so that your disciples also may see the works you are doing; for no one who wants to be widely known acts in secret. If you do these things, show yourself to the world." (For not even his brothers believed in him.) Jesus said to them, "My time has not yet come, but your time is always here. The world cannot hate you, but it hates me because I testify against it that its works are evil. Go to the festival yourselves. I am not going to this festival, for my time has not yet fully come." After saying this, he remained in Galilee.

But after his brothers had gone to the festival, then he also went, not publicly but as it were in secret. The Jews were looking for him at the festival and saying, "Where is he?" And there was considerable complaining about him among the crowds. While some were saying, "He is a good man," others were saying, "No, he is deceiving the crowd." Yet no one would speak openly about him for fear of the Jews.

About the middle of the festival Jesus went up into the temple and began to teach. The Jews were astonished at it, saying, "How does this man have such learning, when he has never been taught?" Then Jesus answered them, "My teaching is not mine, but his who sent me. Anyone who resolves to do the will of God will know whether the teaching is from God or whether I am speaking on my own. Those who speak on their own seek their own glory; but the one who seeks the glory of him who sent him is true, and there is nothing false in him.

"Did not Moses give you the law? Yet none of you keeps the law. Why are you looking for an opportunity to kill me?" The crowd answered, "You have a demon! Who is trying to kill you?" Jesus answered them, "I performed one work, and all of you are astonished. Moses gave you circumcision (it is, of course, not from Moses, but from the patriarchs), and you circumcise a man on the

sabbath. If a man receives circumcision on the sabbath in order that the law of Moses may not be broken, are you angry with me because I healed a man's whole body on the sabbath? Do not judge by appearances, but judge with right judgment."

COMMENTARY

This episode with Jesus' brothers and the festival is a story of intrigue. It is obvious that Jesus' brothers do not believe in him yet, nor are they at all concerned with Jesus' safety. They can't bring themselves to believe that Jesus could be in any more danger than one of them. Jesus, therefore, decides to appear at the festival in a circuitous route, to avoid plans being made against him for capture.

Jesus knew what was being said and planned against him in other parts of the country, and he knew that already he had been targeted for execution. From the first miracle he was a menace, because he stood apart from the world, even while in it.

Jesus' comment to his brothers, "The world cannot hate you," is a judgment upon all of us who think we are related to Christ, but who don't allow "being family" to affect our relationship with the world. On the contrary, to be at peace with Christ means to be at war against the world and its values.

PRAYER 26

Lord Jesus Christ, they were going to try to nip you in the bud. Before your ministry was launched in force, they were going to take you out. So, already, you've learned to move by stealth, showing up when least expected, to avoid an organized trap against you.

Lord, it is difficult for us to identify with that kind of personal danger. We go wherever we want, say whatever we want, and are usually ignored. No one listens to us, and we don't listen to anyone. Our age is an age of insulation. Nothing offends us. We've heard it all. Every side is spoken, and no one gets more than a sound bite on the evening news. It is good you came when you came. You'd make a few talk shows, now, that is all. You'd probably become a little part of a weird parade that fills our minds with the zany and the bizarre.

Lord, we have healers on television now, and almost all the "successful" preachers have a gimmick. We like gimmicks. We like tricks. We like entertainment. How could you be heard in a world like ours?

Lord Jesus Christ, somehow you would find a way to do it. Somehow you would go public with your power again. Somehow you would argue with the leaders, heal the sickly, feed the poor. That would probably be enough to get you in trouble again.

You would take the rich to task. You would show us our sin. You would tell us to simplify our lives. You would get in trouble again.

You would tell our churches to close down the clubhouse. You would tell us to go after the nonbeliever, instead of finding one more way to serve ourselves. You would take away our securities and make us look for your church outside the sanctuary wall. You would be in trouble again.

Lord Jesus Christ, we want to be loved by you in a gentle way. We don't want anything to do with the danger that surrounds you. Like your brothers, we don't see why you don't go public in a nice way. Why stir up the powers that be? Like your brothers, the world doesn't hate us either. Why should they hate us? We are one of them.

Lord, we have thought about being bolder. We have thought about taking a stand, but it's not so easy. It's not just gathering up the courage, it's gathering up the cause, the way, the purpose for which we are willing to risk it all. We are never quite convinced. Someone always shows us the folly of our thinking. Do you know what it's like to have said about you that you have a "martyr complex"? It means that our hearts are not in "the cause," but only in our own personal suffering for "the cause." It's a tricky way to try to earn salvation. It's a way to get attention, not be your person. And perhaps, it is a way that Satan uses to keep us from resolve.

That is the bottom line. You said it yourself in your conclusion: "Anyone who resolves to do the will of God will know whether the teaching is from God or whether I am speaking on my own." Help us gain that resolve.

Lord Jesus Christ, we will never be ready to be your person. We will never be that brave. You know we would like to choose our own destinies. We would like the world to like us, too. Hear these honest confessions of sinful hearts, but fill us with your resolve anyway. Who cares what they say, if you say "this way"? Amen.

27. CHRIST IN OTHERS

John 7:25-36
Now some of the people of Jerusalem were saying, "Is not this the man whom they are trying to kill? And here he is, speaking openly, but they say nothing to him! Can it be that the authorities really know that this is the Messiah? Yet we know where this man is from; but when the Messiah comes, no one will know where he is from." Then Jesus cried out as he was teaching in the temple, "You know me, and you know where I am from. I have not come on my own. But the one who sent me is true, and you do not know him. I know him, because I am from him, and he sent me." Then they tried to arrest him, but no one laid hands on him, because his hour had not yet come. Yet many in the crowd believed in him and were saying, "When the Messiah comes, will he do more signs than this man has done?"

The Pharisees heard the crowd muttering such things about him, and the chief priests and Pharisees sent temple police to arrest him. Jesus then said, "I will be with you a little while longer, and then I am going to him who sent me. You will search for me, but you will not find me; and where I am, you cannot come." The Jews said to one another, "Where does this man intend to go that we will not find him? Does he intend to go to the Dispersion among the Greeks, and teach the Greeks? What does he mean by saying, 'You will search for me and you will not find me' and 'Where I am, you cannot come'?"

COMMENTARY

Two clarifications are made in this passage. First, it is clear that "the hour" that has not yet come is not a reference to the beginning of Jesus' ministry, but the beginning of his passion. Everything leading up to Golgotha is prelude, then begins "the hour."

Secondly, *where* Jesus is from is all linked in with *whom* Jesus is from. He has come from the Father, not so much as an eager volunteer, though that may also be true. He came from the Father "sent."

PRAYER 27

Lord Jesus, there was so much speculation about you even then. Things haven't changed much. Ideas abound, both now and then, regarding your whereabouts, your identity, your words. Sometimes it seems as though ideas about you take the place of you. Sometimes we get weary with what we "think" might be going on in this world, and the next. We weave endless theories and tell endless stories, because we want to inspire one another, but we end up with life as a "tale told by an idiot, signifying nothing."

It is not proof you're trying to establish. You don't seem to be that interested in being very specific about dates and places — just "from the Father." You don't even tell about your miraculous birth, your flight into Egypt, your experience as a boy in the temple. You just say, "I have not come on my own ... I am ... sent."

Lord, we think we have often "gone and done" in your name when we weren't sent. We are so eager to be of help, we jump out in front of your plan, don't bother to consult ... just do. Slow us down, Lord, and help us learn about the One who sent you. Help us want to know all that you've told us about him. Help us understand, like you do, that when he sends us, we will know it — we will not have to suppose it or guess it and hope that it is "our faith" at work. We will be as certain of it as you were.

Lord, you told the people that you were going back to him who sent you, and that they couldn't come with you. Ever since, it seems as though we've been on a hunt to find you. We'll do almost anything to get close to you, the Father, or the Spirit. We'll meditate, brood, think, pray, sing, and sometimes even listen. Yet you and the Father are often remote to us. Even if you are closer than we suppose, even if you are right next to us, if we can't perceive you there, how can we benefit from your nearness? More importantly, perhaps, how can the world benefit from your nearness if it's all invisible?

Yes, Lord, we know that without your constant nearness, our very lives would collapse like a flimsy six-foot water-filled balloon. We know you keep everything supported and alive within our thin skins. We just wish there were a way to see you more clearly, without being annihilated by the experience. Even as we say this, you remind us of your presence among your people, whom we see every day.

Lord, you won't let us just hang on to you, will you, like lint on wool? You keep pushing us into the crowd to find your face. You keep sending us back among one another to share the story. You don't just want us hanging on like leeches. You want us out there discovering your work among others.

Lord, as we find you "out there," may others see in us what we cannot see: your presence within us. They don't have to tell us, because we'll doubt it anyway, and we'll suspect their motive. But, Lord, if you will, bounce some of your light off our lives. You can tell us about it later: where you sent us, what was seen. Much later. Amen.

28. LIVING WATER

John 7:37-52

On the last day of the festival, the great day, while Jesus was standing there, he cried out, "Let anyone who is thirsty come to me, and let the one who believes in me drink. As the scripture has said, 'Out of the believer's heart shall flow rivers of living water.'" Now he said this about the Spirit, which believers in him were to receive; for as yet there was no Spirit, because Jesus was not yet glorified.

When they heard these words, some in the crowd said, "This is really the prophet." Others said, "This is the Messiah." But some asked, "Surely the Messiah does not come from Galilee, does he? Has not the scripture said that the Messiah is descended from David and comes from Bethlehem, the village where David lived?" So there was a division in the crowd because of him. Some of them wanted to arrest him, but no one laid hands on him.

Then the temple police went back to the chief priests and Pharisees, who asked them, "Why did you not arrest him?" The police answered, "Never has anyone spoken like this!" Then the Pharisees replied, "Surely you have not been deceived too, have you? Has any one of the authorities or of the Pharisees believed in him? But this crowd, which does not know the law — they are accursed." Nicodemus, who had gone to Jesus before, and who was one of them, asked, "Our law does not judge people without first giving them a hearing to find out what they are doing, does it?" They replied, "Surely you are not also from Galilee, are you? Search and you will see that no prophet is to arise from Galilee."

COMMENTARY

The contrast between what Jesus says and what the people argue about is glaring once again. The message from Jesus produced conversation about the credentials of Jesus, but not a word about thirst, or living waters, or the Spirit.

It was the temple police that recognized that "Never has anyone spoken like this" — not the chief priests nor the Pharisees.

Even Nicodemus' credibility is challenged, because of his mild defense of Jesus. It is obvious that belief in Jesus is not going to be without consequences.

PRAYER 28

Lord Jesus Christ, what is there about you that brings out the best and the worst in us? How is it that those who spend their lives in search of truth and wisdom find you to be a threat? After all these years to think about it, don't you think it would have been better if you had worked with the religious elite, not against them? They did not see you as a team player.

Of course, we know you are more than a member of a team. You are more coach than quarterback. You are teacher, counselor, and companion searcher. You are the Way, not merely an explorer. You are the stream of living water, not some mud puddle to splash around in.

Lord, we wonder what it means to drink of you. Is "the believer's heart" your heart or ours? Is the water spilled from your side by a soldier's spear while you were on the cross the living water? Is our drinking of you only symbolic, or is it real?

It must be real, Lord, if it's going to quench our thirst for things of the spirit. We will not be satisfied with ideas about you, or ideas about the Spirit or the Father. You know that symbolism is not enough to capture our hearts. We need to taste living, sacrificial water. We need to know the difference between regular water and your water, your life.

Lord, living water scares us. It sounds like it's full of organisms — creepy, crawly things that squirm around inside a body. Living water sounds like it's a step or two beyond just healthy water. If we drink it, will we be different? Yes, you say so.

Lord, you know how much we want to be both safe and spiritual, all in the same moment. You know how much we want to know exactly what you expect of us, in order to measure our own willingness to do your will. We doubt that we can ever let go and drink of you with gusto. You scare us with images like this. You make us think we might drown in raging waters. You make us think we might be swept away forever from our moorings.

But, Lord, we don't like our moorings very much. They are plain and practical and rather boring. We keep ourselves in safe harbor, in very still waters, but we do so with regret, wondering, always wondering, what we would do on the open sea with you along as guide. We think, Lord, we would get lost. We think we would get in big trouble.

So, Lord, what are you to do with these wimpy spirits of ours, except infuse them with your Spirit? If you wait until we are ready, we will never come. If you make us volunteer, we will never do it. Unless you push us and pull us and shame us and love us more than we love ourselves, we will not budge. Budge us, Lord, before we rot on this safe dock of our own making. Love us, Lord, enough to make us drink deeply of you, the living water. Amen.

29. SECOND CHANCE

John 8:1-11

Then each of them went home, while Jesus went to the Mount of Olives. Early in the morning he came again to the temple. All the people came to him and he sat down and began to teach them. The scribes and the Pharisees brought a woman who had been caught in adultery; and making her stand before all of them, they said to him, "Teacher, this woman was caught in the very act of committing adultery. Now in the law Moses commanded us to stone such women. Now what do you say?" They said this to test him, so that they might have some charge to bring against him. Jesus bent down and wrote with his finger on the ground. When they kept on questioning him, he straightened up and said to them, "Let anyone among you who is without sin be the first to throw a stone at her." And once again he bent down and wrote on the ground. When they heard it, they went away, one by one, beginning with the elders; and Jesus was left alone with the woman standing before him. Jesus straightened up and said to her, "Woman, where are they? Has no one condemned you?" She said, "No one, sir." And Jesus said, "Neither do I condemn you. Go your way, and from now on do not sin again."

COMMENTARY

Trying to entrap Jesus, his enemies only provide opportunity for a teaching moment of such consequence that no amount of explanation, from the beginning of time, has covered the matter of judging one another so thoroughly as this event. The trap backfired. Jesus judged the scribes and the Pharisees, instead of the woman.

The woman, on the other hand, never made a confession of guilt or remorse. Jesus, who could know the cunning hearts that brought the woman before him, could also know her heart. It can be a comfort or a fear to have a God so knowledgeable about us that before we confess, he knows what needs to be said.

PRAYER 29

Lord Jesus Christ, I have made many confessions to you, and every one of them was incomplete. You know me so much better than I know myself. Though I try to explain my weaknesses to you, you already know them more thoroughly than I do. If I hide something from you, you know it. If I rationalize my actions, you know it before I do. How can you love sinners like me, so much more vile than our most vivid imaginations can guess? You know us through and through, and love us anyway. Love amazing. Love divine.

Lord, help me love that way. Help me put the stones back into my pockets and see another's pain. Help me to trace my finger through the dust of my critical heart that wants to condemn another, until it touches the soul of the one accused. Help me care for the ones caught in the cycle of sin, instead of worrying about their penalty.

Lord, I cannot begin to imagine what went on in this woman's head as her fate was determined. She claimed no innocence, made no defense, yet she knew that life and death were in the balance for her. She could say nothing to change it. She was there, as we often are, watching events unfold over which we have no control. She was so powerless against the law. She was powerless against her captors. She was able only to be the object of conversation.

Lord, your strength is made perfect in weakness, and if ever there was a better moment to see it happen for another, I don't know where it is in Scripture. You rescued her with quiet words. You saved her from the angry mob with one sentence. You melted the hardness of their hearts by making them look at themselves, instead of at her. She was not the only one saved that day.

Where are our accusers, Lord, if you stand by us? Who can harm us, if you forgive? Even if the stones had been thrown, you would have rescued her. You did not condemn, though you instructed her to sin no more. You gave her another chance, without ignoring the sin. You saw something in her soul worth redeeming. You saw something in the crowd worth challenging. You, Lord, with your finger in the soil, touched the substance from which we all came, and to which we all return. You know firsthand the breath of God breathed into the marvel of human life. You were there at the beginning when body and spirit were united.

Lord, thank you for second chances at life, regardless of our sin, or the opinions of our accusers. Thank you for saving the caught ones. Thank you for rescuing me, when I am caught, in the web of my own undoing.

When I stand before you, convicted, like this woman, have mercy, Lord. Remember the soil from which I came, remember the breath of God, and, in remembering, have mercy, Lord. Have mercy. Amen.

30. HEAVENLY FATHER

John 8:12-30

Again Jesus spoke to them, saying, "I am the light of the world. Whoever follows me will never walk in darkness but will have the light of life." Then the Pharisees said to him, "You are testifying on your own behalf; your testimony is not valid." Jesus answered, "Even if I testify on my own behalf, my testimony is valid because I know where I have come from and where I am going, but you do not know where I come from or where I am going. You judge by human standards; I judge no one. Yet even if I do judge, my judgment is valid; for it is not I alone who judge, but I and the Father who sent me. In your law it is written that the testimony of two witnesses is valid. I testify on my own behalf, and the Father who sent me testifies on my behalf." Then they said to him, "Where is your Father?" Jesus answered, "You know neither me nor my Father. If you knew me, you would know my Father also." He spoke these words while he was teaching in the treasury of the temple, but no one arrested him, because his hour had not yet come.

Again he said to them, "I am going away, and you will search for me, but you will die in your sin. Where I am going, you cannot come." Then the Jews said, "Is he going to kill himself? Is that what he means by saying, 'Where I am going, you cannot come'?" He said to them, "You are from below, I am from above; you are of this world, I am not of this world. I told you that you would die in your sins, for you will die in your sins unless you believe that I am he." They said to him, "Who are you?" Jesus said to them, "Why do I speak to you at all? I have much to say about you and much to condemn; but the one who sent me is true, and I declare to the world what I have heard from him." They did not understand that he was speaking to them about the Father. So Jesus said, "When you have lifted up the Son of Man, then you will realize that I am he, and that I do nothing on my own, but I speak these things as the Father instructed me. And the one who sent me is with me; he has not left me alone, for I always do what is pleasing to him." As he was saying these things, many believed in him.

COMMENTARY

This conversation about being the light of the world and the Father's ambassador is at the heart of Messiahship. Seven times in this passage alone the word "Father" is used. Although "Father" is not to be confused with maleness or earthly fatherhood, the word "Father" is Jesus' own constant choice to name the God of us all. As such, it should not be neglected in our prayers, but receive regular devotional usage, in order to discover the fullness of what it means to call God "Father."

PRAYER 30

Heavenly Father, your son reflected your light. He pointed to you, talked about you, and gave you credit for all that he did. You were his inspiration, his strength, his memory of the place from which he came. More than parent, you were almighty; more than advisor, you were director; more than someone to please, you were companion; more than a cause, you were love; and what you were, you are, and what you are, you shall be, now and always, for us also.

Father, we want to know you as Jesus did. We want to be connected to you as he was. We want you as close as our own heartbeat, within us as breath, as real as our finger's touch. It is through your Son Jesus that we know you best. What he did, he did for you. What he said were words from you. Those whom he called, he called for you. That which he loved above all else was you, Father, more intimate than bone of bone and flesh of flesh. He was of your Spirit, whole and undefiled. He was your walking soul among us. He left your footprints behind, and your words still echo in heart and mind, and your blood still stains the unrepentant life. And what he did, he does, and what he does, he shall do, now and always, for us also.

Father, God of Abraham and Sarah, God of Mohammed, one with Jesus alone, be one with us, too. Infiltrate our lives so thoroughly that we fear nothing but leaving no Father-placed footsteps behind, no Father-given words to remember, no Father-felt sacrifice for another to recognize as your presence still among your people.

It is through Jesus, your Son, and the Holy Spirit that we have been told to work, so send them deep into our beings, penetrate us with your all-invasive love, infiltrate us with a godly amount of courage, and guide us as the author of our lives. Your will be done, on earth by us, as it is done in heaven, by all your holy beings. Your will be done, on earth, by us, dear Father, dearest Heavenly Father, now and always. Amen.

31. HEIRS

John 8:31-38
Then Jesus said to the Jews who had believed in him, "If you continue in my word, you are truly my disciples; and you will know the truth, and the truth will make you free." They answered him, "We are descendants of Abraham and have never been slaves to anyone. What do you mean by saying, 'You will be made free'?"

Jesus answered them, "Very truly, I tell you, everyone who commits sin is a slave to sin. The slave does not have a permanent place in the household; the son has a place there forever. So if the Son makes you free, you will be free indeed. I know that you are descendants of Abraham; yet you look for an opportunity to kill me, because there is no place in you for my word. I declare what I have seen in the Father's presence; as for you, you should do what you have heard from the Father."

COMMENTARY

This passage is all about bondage and slavery, concepts we think we have as little to worry about as the Jews who had come to believe in Jesus. "Slavery," in the physical sense, has not been a part of our recent history, yet "slavery," in the spiritual sense, is as current as today.

We are slaves to sin simply because we can't stop doing it. None of us is able to stop sinning. Regardless of our prayers, our will, our involvement or noninvolvement with others, we cannot escape the shackles of sin. "We are in bondage to sin, and cannot free ourselves." We are, like it or not, part of the human predicament, and there is no escape on earth from that fact.

PRAYER 31

Lord, we are trapped like an animal in a snare, paw caught in a vise from which there is no escape. We see the hunter coming to collect our pelt, club in hand, with no mercy in his eyes. We are not a creature to him, only a pelt, only a skin to be stretched and stacked upon other skins for market; our only value is our outside appearance.

Lord, the world is a snare. It uses up the best years of our lives for so much an hour. We call it "the rat race," the maze from which we cannot escape. It sees only skin-deep, and so we are valued by the quality of our demeanor. But we know that demeanor is a facade, because no one pays for soul, only for production. We feel as though it is economics that guide our way, and we want to eat well and live well. We are afraid to live with less while our neighbor is going after more.

Not all of this is sin, Lord, for you know that we need food, clothing, and shelter. You do not deny us what we need. We may deny others what they need, but you do not deny us, and we do not deny ourselves. Yet, Lord, we remember that you have taught us that life is more than food, and the body is more than clothing. You have taught us that we are spiritual beings, created not only with a body, but with a soul whose origin is your breath. You have taught us to look beyond the physical to the spiritual, beyond the known to the unknown, beyond the logic to the theo-logic, beyond the obvious, the articulate, and the transparent to the mysterious.

Lord, our "mysterious" eyes are dim. We, like Paul, look through a glass darkly. We are not able to see what is coming, or what you would have us do or become. The world is so clear. We know the rules, how to play the game, and how to trap and collect pelts for ourselves. We can win out there. We can escape the snare. We can be free from all worry, except you. We can take care of all matters, except our deaths and their endless aftermaths. We don't know what to do with ourselves after these few brief years at beating the world at its own game, at toying with the world's traps without getting caught.

A thousand souls struggle to take a turn at "success." How senseless it is. Help us before it's too late to escape the world's trap.

To say it in the vernacular, your infinite patience with us is sublime, if not ridiculous. Why do you do it, Lord, except to say that you wish to free us? You say that there are no slaves in your kingdom, only children of the Heavenly Father. You say that there are no pawns, no serfs, no wenches, no traps, just heirs. Who can stand such gospel! Amen.

32. USING FAITH FOREVER

John 8:39-59

They answered him, "Abraham is our father." Jesus said to them, "If you were Abraham's children, you would be doing what Abraham did, but now you are trying to kill me, a man who has told you the truth that I heard from God. This is not what Abraham did. You are indeed doing what your father does." They said to him, "We are not illegitimate children; we have one Father, God himself." Jesus said to them, "If God were your Father, you would love me, for I came from God and now I am here. I did not come on my own, but he sent me. Why do you not understand what I say? It is because you cannot accept my word. You are from your father the devil, and you choose to do your father's desires. He was a murderer from the beginning and does not stand in the truth, because there is no truth in him. When he lies, he speaks according to his own nature, for he is a liar and the father of lies. But because I tell the truth, you do not believe me. Which of you convicts me of sin? If I tell the truth, why do you not believe me? Whoever is from God hears the words of God. The reasons you do not hear them is that you are not from God."

The Jews answered him, "Are we not right in saying that you are a Samaritan and have a demon?" Jesus answered, "I do not have a demon; but I honor my Father, and you dishonor me. Yet I do not seek my own glory; there is one who seeks it and he is the judge. Very truly, I tell you, whoever keeps my word will never see death." The Jews said to him, "Now we know that you have a demon. Abraham died, and so did the prophets; yet you say, 'Whoever keeps my word will never taste death.' Are you greater than our father Abraham, who died? The prophets also died. Who do you claim to be?" Jesus answered, "If I glorify myself, my glory is nothing. It is my Father who glorifies me, he of whom you say, 'He is our God,' though you do not know him. But I know him; if I would say that I do not know him, I would be a liar like you. But I do know him, and I keep his word. Your ancestor Abraham rejoiced that he would see my day; he saw it and was glad." The Jews said to him, "You are not yet fifty years old, and have you seen Abraham?" Jesus said to them, "Very truly, I tell you, before Abraham was, I am." So they picked up stones to throw at him, but Jesus hid himself and went out of the temple.

COMMENTARY

This debate rages around the question, "Who's your father?" There are two possibilities: God or the devil. Because the conversation is accusatory, it produces hostility. Again, Jesus accuses them of wanting to kill him. By the time this passage ends, they are gathering up stones to do just that.

It was the use of the phrase "I am" that drove them to it. They would understand Jesus to be identifying with the God of Moses who said, "I am who I am." This claim would indeed be blasphemous, if it came from anyone other than the Son of God. Without saying, "I am the 'I am' God," Jesus said enough to raise the possibility. For ever after, people must decide whether the Messiah has come in Jesus, or whether they must wait for another. The Father is the one who brings us to the faith that Jesus is the Messiah, and so he glorifies the Son.

PRAYER 32

Lord Jesus Christ, you wouldn't bring the glory upon yourself. You said enough. You wouldn't say, "I am the Messiah, fall down and worship me." You talked mostly about the Father.

How good for you to tell us that you were here before Abraham, that you were with the Father at the beginning of time. By telling us this, we know that hours and days and minutes have no real bearing in your life. How could they? They are measurements of limitations, a way for us to place you in history, but you and the Father are beyond time because you are of the Spirit.

Lord Jesus Christ, so often the question of "When?" is on our hearts and in our minds. We want to know, when are you coming back, when will our problem go away, when will our faith be strong, when will the course be done? We want the calendar filled in, the blueprint of our lives laid out in front of us, the suspense and the mystery gone.

Lord, if you do that, there can be no faith. If you do that, we need no faith, just a detailed script of our individual lives. What good are we to you without faith? It is faith that you want us to develop. You have plans to use our faith forever. You have given to us alone, of all your created creatures, the possibility of faith — a way to see the future, a way to walk in the present with confidence that befuddles Satan himself.

Lord Jesus Christ, you had to do it, too. You had to live by faith that your memory of the former "time" with the Father was real. You had to walk with human feet on solid earth, just like us, and see how stuck in the mud we humans can get. You had to see, firsthand, what a hold Satan has on us, how he mocks your word, makes fun of your message and twists Scripture around to make us want law instead of grace, a path instead of a person, black and white instead of a multitude of colors to show your light. Lord, we would bore ourselves to death, in order to be safe, but you keep turning the prism in your own Father-given light and say, "See this?" "Isn't this different?" "Have you ever thought that this was possible?"

Lord, your questions are better than ours. Your ideas make ours look so puny. You give us a feast, when all we want is hard bread. You give us good wine, when we would be satisfied with stale water. You give us infinite variety, when we would be satisfied with routine.

Lord Jesus Christ, God of infinite opportunity, lift us up to where you are, even as you came down to where we are now. And in that lifting, give us such a view of the world to come, that all our remaining days in this one are spent with restless excitement to be with you forever. Amen.

33. GETTING THE MUD OUT

John 9:1-12

As he walked along, he saw a man blind from birth. His disciples asked him, "Rabbi, who sinned, this man or his parents, that he was born blind?" Jesus answered, "Neither this man nor his parents sinned; he was born blind so that God's works might be revealed in him. We must work the works of him who sent me while it is day; night is coming when no one can work. As long as I am in the world, I am the light of the world." When he had said this, he spat on the ground and made mud with the saliva and spread the mud on the man's eyes, saying to him, "Go, wash in the pool of Siloam" (which means Sent). Then he went and washed and came back able to see. The neighbors and those who had seen him before as a beggar began to ask, "Is this not the man who used to sit and beg?" Some were saying, "It is he." Others were saying, "No, but it is someone like him." He kept saying, "I am the man." But they kept asking him, "Then how were your eyes opened?" He answered, "The man called Jesus made mud, spread it in my eyes, and said to me, 'Go to Siloam and wash.' Then I went and washed and received my sight." They said to him, "Where is he?" He said, "I do not know."

COMMENTARY

This whole chapter in John is devoted to this one healing miracle. The man born blind has character. He will not wilt under powerful crossfire. He knows what happened to him, and he will not be talked out of it.

Jesus could have said, "I must work the works of him who sent me while it is day." He didn't. Instead he said, "We." He said, "We must work the works of him who sent me while it is day." It is a significant statement, because Jesus is sharing the ministry now. He is putting work on us, his disciples. Although it is Jesus' words and power that heal, disciples are participants in the miracle, because they (we!) don't fold under the evidence of God's work among us. The world will make sure that we pay a price for our witness.

PRAYER 33

Lord Jesus, in front of a blind man you announced that you are the light of the world. "A man of the world" would have announced this on a crisp, clear day, from a vantage point where the sighted could see forever. If you were of the world, you would have said it to people who could see, people who could enjoy a vista. Instead you said it in front of a man who had never seen light, never known color, never seen a loved one.

You must have embarrassed your disciples, Jesus, when you talked about being the light of the world in front of that blind man. Although you knew what was going to happen, your disciples didn't. You must understand how nervous we get, as your disciples, when you do things like this. We are cautious because we don't want to hurt peoples' feelings, or promise more in your name than we can deliver. We don't want to be wrong about your intentions. Yes, we will try to work the works of him who sent you while it is day, but Lord, unless you take the lead, we will surely do the wrong works, make bad promises, give false comfort, and be an embarrassment.

You are the light of the world, not just because you say it, but because you bring it. You alone have the power to heal. You alone know the right moment to do it. You waited, God waited, for this miracle, so that it would be written down for all time.

Lord, you didn't get much glory that day. No one seemed very happy with you or with the newly-sighted man. The villagers had walked by him for so many years, they no longer really saw him. They weren't even sure he was the one looking at them! They preferred to hope that it was a case of mistaken identity.

What an embarrassment it would be for a needy person we pass by ever to recognize us. We don't want the poor to see us. We don't want the destitute to know how we live. We don't want the ones we've neglected to have any understanding of how often we've walked by, sneaked by, quietly, because they couldn't see us.

Yet, Lord, you see us. You see what we have and what they need. You know we could at least say a "good morning." We could at least acknowledge the humanness of all who live with a handicap we've been spared. But we, like the herd that settles down after the lion has dropped the antelope, go our way with our day, glad that it was another that must beg for life.

Lord, you are the light, and when we ask for your light, we don't really want it to shine very brightly on our lives, just our path, so we can walk without stumbling. We really don't want to see the opportunities we've missed, nor ones still to come our way. We don't want that much light, Lord. Just a little will do. Just enough for our own safety's sake.

Forgive us, merciful Lord, when we think like this. Open our eyes to see you alive in every human being, so that we may be sent, like the blind man, to wash and get the mud out. Amen.

34. EYES EARTHWARD

John 9:13-41

They brought to the Pharisees the man who had formerly been blind. Now it was a sabbath day when Jesus made the mud and opened his eyes. Then the Pharisees also began to ask him how he had received his sight. He said to them, "He put mud on my eyes. Then I washed, and now I see." Some of the Pharisees said, "This man is not from God, for he does not observe the sabbath." But others said, "How can a man who is a sinner perform such signs?" And they were divided. So they said again to the blind man, "What do you say about him? It was your eyes he opened." He said, "He is a prophet."

The Jews did not believe that he had been blind and had received his sight until they called the parents of the man who had received his sight and asked them, "Is this your son, who you say was born blind? How then does he now see?" His parents answered, "We know that this is our son, and that he was born blind; but we do not know how it is that now he sees, nor do we know who opened his eyes. Ask him; he is of age. He will speak for himself." His parents said this because they were afraid of the Jews; for the Jews had already agreed that anyone who confessed Jesus to be the Messiah would be put out of the synagogue. Therefore his parents said, "He is of age; ask him."

So for the second time they called the man who had been blind, and they said to him, "Give glory to God! We know that this man is a sinner." He answered, "I do not know whether he is a sinner. One thing I do know, that though I was blind, now I see." They said to him, "What did he do to you? How did he open your eyes?" He answered them, "I have told you already, and you would not listen. Why do you want to hear it again? Do you also want to become his disciples?" Then they reviled him, saying, "You are his disciple, but we are disciples of Moses. We know that God has spoken to Moses, but as for this man, we do not know where he comes from." The man answered, "Here is an astonishing thing! You do not know where he comes from, and yet he opened my eyes. We know that God does not listen to sinners, but he does listen to *one who worships him and obeys his will. Never since the world began has it been heard that anyone opened the eyes of a person born blind. If this man were not from God, he could do nothing."* They answered him, *"You were born entirely in sin, and are you trying to teach us?"* And they drove him out.

Jesus heard that they had driven him out, and when he found him, he said, *"Do you believe in the Son of Man?"* He answered, *"And who is he, sir? Tell me, so that I may believe in him."* Jesus said to him, *"You have seen him, and the one speaking with you is he."* He said, *"Lord, I believe."* And he worshiped him. Jesus said, *"I came into this world for judgment so that those who do not see may see, and those who do see may become blind."* Some of the Pharisees near him heard this and said to him, *"Surely we are not blind, are we?"* Jesus said to them, *"If you were blind, you would not have sin. But now that you say, 'We see,' your sin remains."*

COMMENTARY

The world and science want to know "how." The church and faith are concerned with "who." In this miracle story, the questions are mostly about how Jesus successfully did the mud miracle. Even the parents of the healed man are asked the "how" question. The man is twice asked "how" it was done. It is a shallower question, of course, than the "who" question, but by far the more popular. By and large, we don't care who's behind our success, only how to be successful.

But the healed man keeps talking about Jesus, the one, "the who," with the power. The parents, out of fear of the authorities, wouldn't do this. They directed the authorities away from themselves to their very own healed son. When that man did not capitulate under pressure, he was driven out of their presence. When one is healed by God, it's not always an easier road to travel.

PRAYER 34

Lord Jesus Christ, you always seem to be touching the soil. First you draw some letters in the sand, while preparing your answer to those who would have you judge a woman taken in adultery. Now you mix saliva and dirt and make some mud and place it upon already blind eyes. You did not go stargazing when you did miracles. You kept your eyes upon the earth-made people.

Lord, when we are burdened with problems, too often we go off looking for something spooky and ephemeral, rather than physical and enduring. We prefer to hear voices out of the sky, rather than the encouraging word of a God-sent friend. We keep looking for help from visions, while you have a parade of witnesses walk by our faces, each with a story of rescue to tell, each with a word of encouragement to bring.

You came to earth to tell us that earth is where we belong, for a while, for reasons best known to yourself. You came to earth to tell us how to live while here, before the day comes when the physical, truly, is no longer important. Until that day of passing comes, send us to the pool named "Sent" — send us with mud on our eyes if necessary, and with your words in our ears: "Wash your eyes and open them wide, to see whom I've placed in your world for help, and placed in your world to help."

We know, Lord, that it is often easier for us to give help than receive it, because we would not be indebted to anyone. Yet you will not let us live so free and independently. You will not let us be that self-sufficient. You keep jerking us back into the world of human beings and say, "See! Get the mud out of your eyes. Here's my help for you today. I've spent their lifetime directing their steps to your life for this moment. Listen to their care, and if they say the wrong things, forgive them their folly, but remember, I sent them anyway. I sent them to show you I care, even when they do it wrongly."

Thank you, Lord Jesus Christ, for all those people who have the courage to speak a word of love and care to me. Thank you for touching their lives with your healing touch. Thank you for giving them words that comfort and skills that heal. Thank you for bringing us together, out of the love we've learned to share from you, from you alone. Amen.

35. KNOWN BY NAME

John 10:1-10

"*Very truly, I tell you, anyone who does not enter the sheepfold by the gate but climbs in by another way is a thief and a bandit. The one who enters by the gate is the shepherd of the sheep. The gatekeeper opens the gate for him, and the sheep hear his voice. He calls his own sheep by name and leads them out. When he has brought out all his own, he goes ahead of them, and the sheep follow him because they know his voice. They will not follow a stranger, but they will run from him because they do not know the voice of strangers.*" *Jesus used this figure of speech with them, but they did not understand what he was saying to them.*

So again Jesus said to them, "*Very truly, I tell you, I am the gate for the sheep. All who came before me are thieves and bandits; but the sheep did not listen to them. I am the gate. Whoever enters by me will be saved, and will come in and go out and find pasture. The thief comes only to steal and kill and destroy. I came that they may have life, and have it abundantly.*"

COMMENTARY

There is intense imagery in this passage with talk about thieves and bandits, killing and destroying. Through all the turmoil, there is a safe entrance way, known by the gatekeeper. Whether we are coming or going, entering or exiting, it is the voice of the familiar, trustworthy one that gives us confidence that we are being guarded well.

PRAYER 35

Lord Jesus Christ, do you know my name? Are you able to say the syllables that mean *me*? That is what you guarantee in this passage. This is what you say you know. You know us each by name, one by one, regardless of our station in life, and so we follow.

We follow, Lord, because there is no one else to follow like you. We follow because we hear our names. We follow because we hope that you know where we are going, though we do not know ourselves.

Lord, you are very strange, but not a stranger. No one else thinks like you, loves like you, gives like you. You get to us like no one else can. You have in your voice a calming tone, a calling tone, a claiming tone. We are your sheep in your pasture, and nothing can take us over.

What shall we do but look for that narrow slit that is the gateway of life? We cannot find the gate by ourselves because we cannot find you by ourselves. You must show yourself.

You are the gate. You are the key to the gate. You alone grant entrance. You say who goes in and who goes out. You punch the ticket, because you are the ticket. You judge us and know intuitively whether we love you, or eternal life; whether we love you, or what you can do; whether we love you, or whether we are trying to save our own necks. You know us like you know yourself, except we are full of worry and discontent; full of want and feeling guilty for it; full of hope, but wondering, always, if we have bet on the right gate.

Lord, we are "fools" for you. No other word says it so bluntly and so honestly. We are your people because you know our names, individually, one by one. We are your people because you alone know the way into the sheepfold, the way to live while here, and the way out to eternal life. We are your people because we are irresistibly drawn to love, drawn to you, the key, the gate, the gatekeeper, the calling voice we trust. Amen.

36. SLIPPING OVER CLIFFS

John 10:11-21
"I am the good shepherd. The good shepherd lays down his life for the sheep. The hired hand, who is not the shepherd and does not own the sheep, sees the wolf coming and leaves the sheep and runs away — and the wolf snatches them and scatters them. The hired hand runs away because a hired hand does not care for the sheep. I am the good shepherd. I know my own and my own know me, just as the Father knows me and I know the Father. And I lay down my life for the sheep. I have other sheep that do not belong to this fold. I must bring them also, and they will listen to my voice. So there will be one flock, one shepherd. For this reason the Father loves me, because I lay down my life in order to take it up again. No one takes it from me, but I lay it down of my own accord. I have power to lay it down, and I have power to take it up again. I have received this command from my Father."

Again the Jews were divided because of these words. Many of them were saying, "He has a demon and is out of his mind. Why listen to him?" Others were saying, "These are not the words of one who has a demon. Can a demon open the eyes of the blind?"

COMMENTARY

This is another one of seven "I am" sayings spoken by Jesus and recorded by John. The picture of Jesus as the good shepherd has graced the halls of many church school rooms, where the perilous sheep, caught in a thicket by the cliff, is about to fall or be rescued. It is a fitting image. The imperiled sheep has no possibility of wandering back to the fold without help. Only a Good Shepherd can initiate and complete a rescue.

As we think we are making our own way back to the fold of faith, it is really God behind us, pushing us with his staff, or God in front of us, pulling us with his crook. When it's all done, we know it was Christ beside us, coaxing us every step of the way.

PRAYER 36

Lord Jesus Christ, someone is certainly out of his mind. Either it is you for leading so many innocent people astray, or it is the world, for preferring to save itself from the precipitous cliff after having wandered over the ledge. How we want to scramble back up to safety by ourselves. How we want to lift ourselves up by our own bootstraps. How we pretend to have done it, even when it was you who restored us and saved us.

You take much verbal abuse by being a Savior. Your name is not respected by those who think no one is in control, or that they are in control. As they mock you, they mock us who believe in you. Still, you keep after all of us, ever trying to fix us permanently into your way.

Good Shepherd Jesus, I don't want to be a sheep, an animal. I want to be like you, full of wisdom and power, able to solve all problems with a word or a touch. Given the choice, almost all of us would choose to live by strength, not grace, for we love to lead, love to be in control, love to be successful. What are you doing to us by calling us sheep?

We know it is true. We know that we are not that lovable little wooly lamb, so clean and pure a few days after birth, but rather a dirty, old, smelly, mud-caked sheep, unable to find pasture, shelter from a storm, or even purpose for living without you. What do you see in us, Lord? We humans don't even have wool to offer you. It is even expensive to dispose of our carcasses.

Good Shepherd Jesus, I have tried too hard to be someone other than what you've made me. Either I have wanted to be like you, just as Eve and Adam wanted to be like you, or I have wanted to be like the beasts of the field, without responsibility to anyone or anything. But you made me in your image, not to take your place, but to be your person, and to grow differently from all the other creatures you have made. You made me to be a recipient of a grace so vibrant as to be life itself. When you breathed into me, you gave me soul. When you breathed into me, you gave me heart. You altered this animal body and made essence possible, love real.

From love you made us for love. You've given no other creature, physical or spiritual, so much love. No other creature has so much at risk. We have bodies to lose, and we know it. We have pain to suffer in our bodies, and we know it. We have such limited knowledge of how vast and incomprehensible the world is that you made, and we know it. We have such a short time to become your person, and we know it. We are forever slipping over cliffs, sometimes on purpose, and we know it.

Good Shepherd Jesus, you know us, too. You know us better than we know ourselves. You know our need is desperate. You pour grace upon grace upon us.

Good Shepherd Jesus, shepherd me. From behind, goad me with your staff when I am lazy or wandering. From out front, pull me with your shepherd's crook, because the way looks dark and rocky. But most especially, call my name softly, so that I may know it is you at my side, and not another. I am your sheep and your intimate. I am your problem and your lover. Good Shepherd, be good to me, because I need you more than you need me. Amen.

37. NEVER ALONE

John 10:22-42

At that time the festival of the Dedication took place in Jerusalem. It was winter, and Jesus was walking in the temple, in the portico of Solomon. So the Jews gathered around him and said to him, "How long will you keep us in suspense?" Jesus answered, "I have told you, and you do not believe. The works that I do in my Father's name testify to me; but you do not believe, because you do not belong to my sheep. My sheep hear my voice. I know them, and they follow me. I give them eternal life, and they will never perish. No one will snatch them out of my hand. What my Father has given me is greater than all else, and no one can snatch it out of the Father's hand. The Father and I are one."

The Jews took up stones again to stone him. Jesus replied, "I have shown you many good works from the Father. For which of these are you going to stone me?" The Jews answered, "It is not for a good work that we are going to stone you, but for blasphemy, because you, though only a human being, are making yourself God." Jesus answered, "Is it not written in your law, 'I said, you are gods'? If those to whom the word of God came were called 'gods' — and the scripture cannot be annulled — can you say that the one whom the Father has sanctified and sent into the world is blaspheming because I said, 'I am God's Son'? If I am not doing the works of my Father, then do not believe me. But if I do them, even though you do not believe me, believe the works, so that you may know and understand that the Father is in me and I am in the Father." Then they tried to arrest him again, but he escaped from their hands. He went away again across the Jordan to the place where John had been baptizing earlier, and he remained there. Many came to him, and they were saying, "John performed no sign, but everything that John said about this man was true." And many believed in him there.

COMMENTARY

Jesus' claims can be no larger than these. He was clearly saying that he was the Messiah, but more than the Messiah. He was the Son of the Heavenly Father, sent and commissioned, and "at one" with the Father God. In other words, what is his, is the Father's, and vice versa. What he is, is Father-like, and what the Father is, is Son-like.

It was not just the ears of his opponents that were offended by this. It was their love of the rigid Father God, as best they understood him, that led them to challenge this audacious claim. Every good orthodox person worth a grain of salt knows that dragging one's feet *is* the right thing to do 99 percent of the time. Heresies, like dandelions, will bloom in any sunny place.

There are two complementary dual "ownerships" in this passage. The first is between Jesus and us. Jesus, the Good Shepherd, knows us; we also know the Good Shepherd. We recognize each other's voice.

The second dual ownership is between the Son and the Father. That which is given to Jesus cannot be snatched out of the "Father's" hand. What and who belongs to Christ, belongs also and equally to the Father.

PRAYER 37

Lord Jesus, talking with you is talking with the Father who sent you. The two of you are one in the Spirit, one in fact. Nothing separates you. You are more than the Father's ambassador, more than his "sent one." You are also united as one, inseparable forever, a unity of will and purpose, a team with but a single player.

Lord Jesus, Shepherd, we need to train our ears to hear your voice. We sense that you are always near, whispering in our ears, but the din of the world and our own constant needs are deafening madness. We cannot get away from the world even when we are alone, for the world travels with us with its cares and concerns. We have a hundred "I's" in every prayer. Every time we think we hear your voice, we doubt it at once, wondering about the "soundness" of such a thought. We have institutions for people who hear your voice too easily, who think they have you tuned in directly. We make jokes about them, because what they hear, we think, are the desires of their own minds and hearts, but not your voice.

Sometimes, Lord, you speak words that are not comforting. Those are very hard words to hear. Sometimes you speak words of judgment and hurt our feelings. Sometimes you goad and challenge; sometimes you stroke and assure. You will be what you will be, and you will say what you will say. We all prefer you to be gentle, but a Good Shepherd won't let the sheep get fat and lazy.

Lord, as you direct our paths, help us walk confidently, like one who is not alone. When we tire, encourage us with your strength. When we balk at the steepness of the hill, push us. When it's dark and we can't see, pull us, because we want you out ahead. When we come across a place to rest, may your shoulder be our pillow. When there is time to enjoy a vista, may your words direct our eyes to the most beautiful point. When we fall down, catch us. When we die, embrace us in your arms. When we awake, be by our graves, calling in a voice we'll recognize as yours and yours alone. Then it will be time to meet our Father together. Amen.

38. BE THE LIGHT

John 11:1-16

Now a certain man was ill, Lazarus of Bethany, the village of Mary and her sister Martha. Mary was the one who anointed the Lord with perfume and wiped his feet with her hair; her brother Lazarus was ill. So the sisters sent a message to Jesus, "Lord, he whom you love is ill." But when Jesus heard it, he said, "This illness does not lead to death; rather it is for God's glory, so that the Son of God may be glorified through it." Accordingly, though Jesus loved Martha and her sister and Lazarus, after having heard that Lazarus was ill, he stayed two days longer in the place where he was.

Then after this he said to the disciples, "Let us go to Judea again." The disciples said to him, "Rabbi, the Jews were just now trying to stone you, and are you going there again?" Jesus answered, "Are there not twelve hours of daylight? Those who walk during the day do not stumble, because they see the light of this world. But those who walk at night stumble, because the light is not in them." After saying this, he told them, "Our friend Lazarus has fallen asleep, but I am going there to awaken him." The disciples said to him, "Lord, if he has fallen asleep, he will be all right." Jesus, however, had been speaking about his death, but they thought that he was referring merely to sleep. Then Jesus told them plainly, "Lazarus is dead. For your sake I am glad I was not there, so that you may believe. But let us go to him." Thomas, who was called the Twin, said to his fellow disciples, "Let us also go, that we may die with him."

COMMENTARY

Thomas knew it intuitively: more dangerous business. Jesus, for the sake of a friend and the glory of God, was willing to go back to Bethany, where they had tried to stone him to death. Now he was going back into the arena of adversaries, who still had itching hands to throw the first stone.

The reason for Jesus' delay to visit his friend is not given. Whenever God doesn't answer us as promptly as we wish, we may wonder, "What's so important that I must wait for God's action on my behalf?" This time the delay was for our sake, that we may believe. Even after decay has begun, Jesus can restore. This becomes much more than a mere awakening. This is a raising and a restoration, and no one would ever be able to forget it.

PRAYER 38

Lord, your disciples warned you with an urgency that is almost humorous: "Just now," they said, "the Jews were trying to stone you." "Just now," Lord, had to be at least a few days ago, but it seemed to the disciples like only a moment away. They were still excited about it, pumped up, looking over their shoulders to see who was approaching. They were scared, Lord, pure and simple, when you said, "Let us go to Judea again."

You talk about daylight, Lord, as helpful for only twelve hours a day. After that, without an outside source of light, we stumble, because the light is not within us. You imply, Lord, that you have a light within that keeps you from stumbling. You are that light, as real as the light that shines in the daytime. You see in the dark because you are the light that overcomes the darkest darkness of this world.

You knew what you were going to do. You knew that Lazarus was dead and buried in a dark, cold tomb. You knew it was too late for healing. Perhaps you didn't bother to tell your disciples exactly what you planned to do because they would have left you all alone. Which one of us could have followed you back to the place where they were ready to stone you for healing a blind man? If you had said, "Come, and watch me raise Lazarus from the dead," we all would have fled for sanity's sake, or in fear, or walked away bewildered and sad that you had made a pompous claim over the finality of death itself.

Lord, death's darkness is still faith's sticking point. Many cannot come to believe that you have this much power over us. Perhaps like a doctor, you can delay it, but not overcome it. Besides, there is always another way to explain the raising of the dead. Theories abound from fertile imaginations. They did then, and they do now. In the end, Lord, there is no proof possible. Proof and faith, like oil and water, do not mix. Proof becomes the enemy of faith. Proof makes faith disappear by making faith unnecessary.

So, now you are ready to really light up dark eyes. Now you are going to do the deed that will live in infamy among your enemies. Now you will cast the lots that cannot be taken back. Now they will seek to darken you for good, put out your lights forever, end this nonsense once and for all.

Lord, I am with your disciples now, trembling in fear. You are about to bring disaster upon us all. You are about to change the history of the world if you are successful, or cause much laughter if you are not. Either way, as your people, we are marked for slaughter or ridicule.

Do it anyway, Lord. Let the powers that be see their limitations for a change. Cast out the great darkness. Be the light of the world. Open the eyes of a dead man. And, when he sees, may we see the powers of this world withdraw in fear and awe before you. Amen.

39. OPENING DEATH'S DARK EYES

John 11:17-27

When Jesus arrived, he found that Lazarus had already been in the tomb four days. Now Bethany was near Jerusalem, some two miles away, and many of the Jews had come to Martha and Mary to console them about their brother. When Martha heard that Jesus was coming, she went and met him, while Mary stayed at home. Martha said to Jesus, "Lord, if you had been here, my brother would not have died. But even now I know that God will give you whatever you ask of him." Jesus said to her, "Your brother will rise again." Martha said to him, "I know that he will rise again in the resurrection on the last day." Jesus said to her, "I am the resurrection and the life. Those who believe in me, even though they die, will live, and everyone who lives and believes in me will never die. Do you believe this?" She said to him, "Yes, Lord, I believe that you are the Messiah, the Son of God, the one coming into the world."

COMMENTARY

Martha's declaration of faith preceded Jesus' action with Lazarus. She is "proof" that true faith precedes "proof." She was where we are. She had no more reason to believe that Christ was the Messiah than do we. In many ways, she had much less "reason," for she was still on the other side of the resurrection of Jesus, and Lazarus still lay buried in the tomb. It was not his raising that provoked faith. It was Christ alone.

PRAYER 39

Jesus Christ, when we are with you alone, you are irresistible. You mesmerize us with your Spirit. You infiltrate us like air in our lungs. You are our all in all, and there is no place to hide, no way to run. You stop all exits from appearing. You block our escape into reason. One look from you at us and our hearts melt, like the young in love.

Lord, because all of this is true, we avoid you, too. You are too much. You are the infinite filling up the finite. You are blinding light, searing truth, bursting all our capacity to hold you in. You are the tidal wave upon the beach, the cyclone in the desert, the flood in the valley. When you arrive, you overcome us.

We avoid you, Lord, because of this. Who wants to be so out of control? Who dares sink in a love deeper than the ocean with a mere promise that you will catch us? Who has the courage to say with Martha, "You are the one. You are God upon the earth"? To do so radically changes all we think and do, and so we avoid you.

You are dangerous, Lord. You sweep us away with your energy. You confound all the values of the world. You rearrange our priorities quicker than we can list our dreams. You turn everything upside down and inside out, because you are not of this world. You don't belong here anymore. You need to go to the Father and live where it's safe for you to be.

Yet, Lord, if you go and leave us alone, what shall we be? We have caught a glimpse of your glory, and we have heard of your way. Without you, our hearts will be homesick, our yearnings will be fierce, our restlessness will be too intense to endure.

You are the resurrection and the life. You are creator God and lover God. We cannot live or love without you. To avoid you is to perish. So, Lord God Jesus Christ, open up the death-dark eyes in each of us, enough to know the way to you. Amen.

40. CRY FOR US

John 11:28-44

When she had said this, she went back and called her sister Mary, and told her privately, "The Teacher is here and is calling for you." And when she heard it, she got up quickly and went to him. Now Jesus had not yet come to the village, but was still at the place where Martha had met him. The Jews who were with her in the house, consoling her, saw Mary get up quickly and go out. They followed her because they thought that she was going to the tomb to weep there. When Mary came where Jesus was and saw him, she knelt at his feet and said to him, "Lord, if you had been here, my brother would not have died." When Jesus saw her weeping, and the Jews who came with her also weeping, he was greatly disturbed in spirit and deeply moved. He said, "Where have you laid him?" They said to him, "Lord, come and see." Jesus began to weep. So the Jews said, "See how he loved him!" But some of them said, "Could not he who opened the eyes of the blind man have kept this man from dying?"

Then Jesus, again greatly disturbed, came to the tomb. It was a cave, and a stone was lying against it. Jesus said, "Take away the stone." Martha, the sister of the dead man, said to him, "Lord, already there is a stench because he has been dead four days." Jesus said to her, "Did I not tell you that if you believed, you would see the glory of God?" So they took away the stone. And Jesus looked upward, and said, "Father, I thank you for having heard me. I knew that you always hear me, but I have said this for the sake of the crowd standing here, so that they may believe that you sent me." When he had said this, he cried with a loud voice, "Lazarus, come out!" The dead man came out, his hands and feet bound with strips of cloth, and his face wrapped in a cloth. Jesus said to them, "Unbind him, and let him go."

COMMENTARY

Both Martha and Mary say the same thing to Jesus: "If you had been here, Lazarus would not have died." Both of them knew that Jesus had power to heal, and both were of the opinion that Jesus would have performed a miracle to save Lazarus. Jesus' delay gave need for a much greater miracle than a healing.

The grief of Jesus is intense. Twice we are told that he was "greatly disturbed." Even though he knew what could be done about this death, he grieved, because the mortality of Lazarus was evident, both now and again later. This grieving by Jesus is so important, because he felt what we feel when a loved one dies. He felt the anguish, could see the pain, feel the separation, know firsthand what it is to lose a friend.

PRAYER 40

Lord, you stood and shouted for all to hear: "Lazarus, come out." You didn't shout so the dead could hear. You could have talked to the dead with a whisper, and who could argue that you did it? You shouted aloud for us, so that we might believe that this was no hocus-pocus magic, but your Word alone doing wonders. You shouted it before you had a chance to see "if it would work." You risked your whole ministry, and an already great reputation, on something new and untried, on something old and emitting a stench. You shouted out in faith, and Lazarus got up.

We wonder, Lord, how hard it was for Lazarus to come back into this world. We wonder how the rest of his life was lived, and how his second dying occurred. We wonder what, if anything, he left behind by coming back. You don't tell us, and it doesn't matter, because your message is more important than Lazarus' feelings or losses. You did this, not just for Martha, Mary, and Lazarus, whom you loved. You did this to send a warning shot across the bow of Satan. You did this for us.

Lord, you are the right one to have on our side. If death cannot stand before you, we have nothing to fear. If all our enemies' legs are molasses, the worst they can do is temporary. They can fill us with misery, but only for a while. They can make us dread our daily fare, but only for a while. They can inflict pain and take joy out of this life, but compared to eternity, it is only for a while. You have the last word, because you had the first word. As the Alpha and Omega, you are the beginning and the end, the life and the resurrection.

Lord of power and might, you who can regenerate human flesh with a word, you who can restore the broken family on earth and in heaven, you who feel our sorrow: cry for us as you did with them when our tears dry up. When no earthly words are left for us to express our pain and rage, may we have the pleasure of hearing you sob? May we know that you love us as deeply as you loved them, and that your Spirit groans for us with sighs too deep for words when life is wrenched away?

Lord, what we need from you is the assurance, the simple assurance, that our grief is not being done in a vacuum, but is joined by you and the company of heaven. What we need from you is no simple, "Everything's going to be all right, eventually." What we need from you is what you gave to Martha and Mary and Lazarus' friends. We need your passion and compassion, the pleasure of your shared and broken heart, your arm on our shoulder and your tears mingling with ours. Then, truly, you are the God of mercy, whose day of resurrection will come with a joy no enemy can spoil. Then, Lord of the Resurrection, your joy and victory will be real, and no mere game against the enemies. Then, Lord, we will join together in mutual celebration, for both your suffering and our sufferings will have ended. Amen.

41. ANY ONE OF US

John 11:45-57

Many of the Jews therefore, who had come with Mary and had seen what Jesus did, believed in him. But some of them went to the Pharisees and told them what he had done. So the chief priests and the Pharisees called a meeting of the council, and said, "What are we to do? This man is performing many signs. If we let him go on like this, everyone will believe in him, and the Romans will come and destroy both our holy place and our nation." But one of them, Caiaphas, who was high priest that year, said to them, "You know nothing at all! You do not understand that it is better for you to have one man die for the people than to have the whole nation destroyed." He did not say this on his own, but being high priest that year he prophesied that Jesus was about to die for the nation, and not for the nation only, but to gather into one the dispersed children of God. So from that day on they planned to put him to death.

Jesus therefore no longer walked about openly among the Jews, but went from there to a town called Ephraim in the region near the wilderness; and he remained there with his disciples.

Now the Passover of the Jews was near, and many went up from the country to Jerusalem before the Passover to purify themselves. They were looking for Jesus and were asking one another as they stood in the temple, "What do you think? Surely he will not come to the festival, will he?" Now the chief priests and the Pharisees had given orders that anyone who knew where Jesus was should let them know, so that they might arrest him.

COMMENTARY

The nation was at stake. So were the holy places. Jesus was a threat both to Rome and Israel, simply because Rome would not tolerate anyone becoming more popular than the emperor. The leaders were running on fear, and fear produced great mistakes in judgment. The high priest made a prophecy (doubtlessly his one and only!) the likes of which even he wasn't remotely aware. Yes, Jesus would die for the nation, but for much more than a single nation.

Meanwhile, as all of this intrigue was happening, the people were ready for more drama. They could hardly wait to see if Jesus would show. Someone was probably making odds on it for betting purposes. The word was out that he would be arrested on sight.

The scene behind the scene behind the scene is the master plan. God had set the stage for the historical events to happen that would gather together all "the dispersed children of God." Which, of course, means us.

PRAYER 41

Lord Jesus, you should have stayed in Ephraim. Why risk your ministry's duration on the expectations of the people? Why go to Jerusalem and risk capture? Think of all the good you could yet do. Think of the people who could benefit from your touch, the stories you could tell, the doctrine you could explain. Think of the bigger crowds to come, the organization you could found. Why, with some good planning, in a few years you might take Rome.

Maybe you had some of those thoughts, Lord. We don't know. We do know that you didn't give them much consideration. You and the Father had set your face to Jerusalem. You knew the time had come. And, because your hour had come, the time of history was split in two, before and after yourself.

Lord, think of the people waiting there for you. Many were cruel and willing to kill. Many others were merely curiosity seekers, ready for a good show. Most probably didn't care one way or the other. You would be a matinee at most, a diversion for the season, something to do to break the monotony of the festival, like something special in church on Sunday morning. That's all. Think of it, Lord. Think.

When we think like this we know why you once called Peter "Satan." We are all natural tempters of you, Lord. We see clear danger out there, danger to you and danger to us. But the real weakness in us, Lord, is that we don't see us worth the risk. We think that most other people are just like us. We are not worth it, Lord. We are unworthy of another's death, especially yours. We don't see how you can do it for the likes of us.

Lord, this is what makes you Lord. You have a love beyond our own for each of us. You say, "I think more highly of you than you do for yourself, more highly of your neighbor than your neighbor believes possible."

Lord, you have placed a value on us that no reasonable person would place. The world says that Caiaphas was right. He speaks our language. What does it matter if one person dies for a nation? But you, Lord, would die for just one of us. Any one of us. No matter what we've done or become. Any one of us.

Remind us, Lord, that behind the obvious, the quick fix, the simple solution, you are at work on a master plan. Remind us, Lord, that we have become the object of that master plan because we are the object of your affection. How it changes us when we think about it! No more groveling, Lord. You love us; you love me. No more false modesty. We're each worth a lot; I'm worth a lot. I've been died for. You would have done it if I were the only one needing a Savior. I've been died for by the King. Amen.

42. TIME AT HIS FEET

John 12:1-8

Six days before the Passover Jesus came to Bethany, the home of Lazarus, whom he had raised from the dead. There they gave a dinner for him. Martha served, and Lazarus was one of those at the table with him. Mary took a pound of costly perfume made of pure nard, anointed Jesus' feet, and wiped them with her hair. The house was filled with the fragrance of the perfume. But Judas Iscariot, one of his disciples (the one who was about to betray him), said, "Why was this perfume not sold for three hundred denarii and the money given to the poor?" (He said this not because he cared about the poor, but because he was a thief; he kept the common purse and used to steal what was put into it.) Jesus said, "Leave her alone. She bought it so that she might keep it for the day of my burial. You always have the poor with you, but you do not always have me."

COMMENTARY

Judas, Lazarus, and Mary are all intertwined in this text. Judas cared little about the poor or Jesus. Collecting money was his specialty, and like many other persons, there was never quite enough of it on deposit to make him feel secure. Additionally, he was a thief.

Lazarus knows that being the object of a miracle of Jesus puts one in a dangerous position, especially if one isn't quiet about it. If Lazarus were smart, he would go to a distant land, raise tomatoes, and be inwardly grateful to be alive. However, he did much more. He became known. Many believed because of him.

Mary anoints Jesus' feet not as a simple gesture of servitude, but as recognition of him as Messiah. She has seen beyond the great arena of service to Christ, to the greater arena of being in the presence of God. That difference is most difficult for us to comprehend, because the mysterious presence of "God with us" has been diluted by a simpler duty of giving and receiving service to and from one another in the name of Christ. Prayer may help us understand.

PRAYER 42

Lord Jesus, everyone who comes into your life brings consequences. Judas' true nature is found out, Lazarus becomes a target to be murdered, and Mary, who knows who you really are, is criticized for her devotion. Sometimes it seems it would be better never to learn a thing about you, or to follow you for more than a moment.

Judas, Lord, must have been a painful case for you. Here was a man who had every opportunity to come into the faith, but his love for money was greater than all. He is such a pathetic man, because he has no vision. He cannot see whom he is with. He can only see money.

Lazarus, Lord, loved you enough to cause you to weep over his death. Was it a favor to bring him back into this world? Did you do it for him or for us? Were you just doing what God does best by restoring life? You use us, Lord, even when it doesn't suit us. You use us to show your power. You must have this privilege if your will is to be done, on earth, as in heaven.

Mary saw you most clearly, Lord. She didn't see feet that needed anointing when she looked at you. She saw God in your eyes, love in your heart, the Messiah upon earth. For her to be true she had no choice but to fall at your feet with anointing oil. Like the wise man at your birth, bringing the gift of myrrh, now it is administered in love by the wisest of women in preparation for your burial.

Lord, with that oil and kneeling, Mary proclaimed to all of us the mysterious presence of a sacrificing God among us. She wasn't denying the plight of the miserable poor, but only indicating that she knew you were going to die.

Mary showed us, Lord, that time at your feet is essential. If we see you rightly, dying like the poor and forsaken, won't we also see the poor as our poor? You know that if we kneel rightly before you, when we rise we will no longer serve one another begrudgingly.

Lord, she saw you dying for her as she knelt before you. She saw your burial coming, your sacrifice, for her. She saw herself as a sinner who needed a Savior. And although she couldn't see your resurrection yet, she knew that being died for by you was more important than anything else on earth.

Lord, help us see that we cannot serve our neighbor rightly without first kneeling at your feet. Help us see that we cannot stop worrying about our own sin until we see the price you paid to make it have no more power to separate us from one another. Help us see what Mary saw when she saw you. Help us see you now, almighty God. Amen.

43. BEING DIED FOR BY THE MESSIAH

John 12:9-26

When the great crowd of the Jews learned that he was there, they came not only because of Jesus but also to see Lazarus, whom he had raised from the dead. So the chief priests planned to put Lazarus to death as well, since it was on account of him that many of the Jews were deserting and were believing in Jesus.

The next day the great crowd that had come to the festival heard that Jesus was coming to Jerusalem. So they took branches of palm trees and went out to meet him, shouting, "Hosanna! Blessed is the one who comes in the name of the Lord — the King of Israel!"

Jesus found a young donkey and sat on it; as it is written: "Do not be afraid, daughter of Zion. Look, your king is coming, sitting on a donkey's colt!" His disciples did not understand these things at first; but when Jesus was glorified, then they remembered that these things had been written of him and had been done to him. So the crowd that had been with him when he called Lazarus out of the tomb and raised him from the dead continued to testify. It was also because they heard that he had performed this sign that the crowd went to meet him. The Pharisees then said to one another, "You see, you can do nothing. Look, the world has gone after him!"

Now among those who went up to worship at the festival were some Greeks. They came to Philip, who was from Bethsaida in Galilee, and said to him, "Sir, we wish to see Jesus." Philip went and told Andrew; then Andrew and Philip went and told Jesus. Jesus answered them, "The hour has come for the Son of Man to be glorified. Very truly, I tell you, unless a grain of wheat falls into the earth and dies, it remains just a single grain; but if it dies, it bears much fruit. Those who love their life lose it, and those who hate their life in this world will keep it for eternal life. Whoever serves me must follow me, and where I am, there will my servant be also. Whoever serves me, the Father will honor."

COMMENTARY

The plots to kill have doubled. Jesus and Lazarus are both targets. Assassination is a strategy solution of the world whenever someone in the world wanders away from the gods established by itself. The raising of Lazarus from the dead took the minds and hearts of the people away from the customs of the day. The people were curious, the Lazarus witnesses bold, the Hosanna pep rally too big to control. It was too dangerous a time to make the move to kill them both because, for one brief day, the world was looking in the right direction.

That Jesus had to die, if ever we were to come to faith, is one of the most difficult things we have to welcome, not just learn. We don't want to believe that his death was that necessary for us, at least not individually. Yet it was and is. If any one of us were the only person on earth, he would have been crucified for us alone ... any ONE of us.

We are the Greeks in this text who come to Philip and say, "Sir, we would see Jesus." When Jesus hears of it, he knows that all the world is ready for the Someone who can raise the dead. He also knows that all the world was not ready either to see him die a cruel death, or to believe that it was necessary for it to occur for our own sake, our own individual sake.

PRAYER 43

Lord Jesus Christ, I can hardly understand it. Your dying as God, for the sake of an animal person like me, seems to be too much love, too much unnecessary suffering. It seems like "overkill." I can hardly think it was necessary. I do not like to take it all that personally. I much prefer that you die for all of us corporately, rather than for me individually. Perhaps all of humankind is worth it, but not I.

You did not do it, did you, because I was worth it? You did not do it because you had faith that someday I would understand it. You did it because I needed it, more than breath itself. You did it to win me from the one who would tell me that it wasn't necessary, from the one who would say that I really wasn't worth it. You did it to win me from the one who thinks less of me than you do. Why does his evil logic sound so true?

Lord, when I try to enthrone you, as the people singing you into Jerusalem did, you keep backing away into the crowd and closer to the cross. I lose sight of you. Between your enemies who would kill you, because you distracted people like me from their leadership, and your own unwillingness to be the king of this world, figuring out how to safely grab hold of you is a slippery task. As soon as I would box you in and put you on a shelf to admire, you jump away, and near the cross.

All of my life, Lord, I have sought to play it safe, keep out of trouble, learn the rules, and be successful. All my life, Lord, you keep sending me troubles. If you don't send them, they arrive anyway. I keep trying to find out how to nest with you, and you keep pushing me out, from dizzying heights, not with a command to fly, but with a promise that you'll catch me. Why, Lord, do you want me to do this? What if I jump at the wrong time? What if my own need to prove my faithfulness is really the motivating factor, and not your call to trust you? Unless you push me, I won't go. I know it.

Lord, I can count the years and know that mine are drawing to a close. I know that I cannot save my life in this world or gain entrance into the next without you. I know that you value faith in your presence and Way above all else, and I know that your Way involves the cross. So, that is my hesitation. I've had enough suffering. I don't want to go out looking for it. I don't want to be called upon to endure more of it. I don't want to call upon others to do more of it and say to them, "What did you expect, if you were going to follow the Lord?" Don't you know, Lord, that honey draws more flies than vinegar?

Was it vinegar, Lord, that they put on hyssop and held to your lips on the cross?

The world and I want the fruits of the Spirit, the peace, joy, comfort, and love that you promise. We don't want a cross. We don't want to die like a thief. We don't want our loved ones to die. We don't want you to die either.

Lord, when will I be your person? When will I get over my dread of death and "fear it as little as my bed"? When will you be such a part of my life that my eternal life will have already begun? I am one reluctant servant. I am Jonah all over again.

In the words of the Gospel of John that are yet to be prayed over, Lord Jesus Christ, come and mold me anew. I don't like being so afraid of death, of the future, or of aloneness. Show me the power of your cross. Do more than show me, if necessary, but do it gently, Lord. I am not so brave. Amen.

44. OFF BALANCE, BUT PIOUS?

John 12:27-43

"Now my soul is troubled. And what should I say — 'Father, save me from this hour'? No, it is for this reason that I have come to this hour. Father, glorify your name." Then a voice came from heaven, "I have glorified it, and I will glorify it again." The crowd standing there heard it and said that it was thunder. Others said, "An angel has spoken to him." Jesus answered, "This voice has come for your sake, not for mine. Now is the judgment of this world; now the ruler of this world will be driven out. And I, when I am lifted up from the earth, will draw all people to myself." He said this to indicate the kind of death he was to die. The crowd answered him, "We have heard from the law that the Messiah remains forever. How can you say that the Son of Man must be lifted up? Who is this Son of Man?" Jesus said to them, "The light is with you for a little longer. Walk while you have the light, so that the darkness may not overtake you. If you walk in the darkness, you do not know where you are going. While you have the light, believe in the light, so that you may become children of light."

After Jesus had said this, he departed and hid from them. Although he had performed so many signs in their presence, they did not believe in him. This was to fulfill the word spoken by the prophet Isaiah: "Lord, who has believed our message, and to whom has the arm of the Lord been revealed?" And so they could not believe, because Isaiah also said, "He has blinded their eyes and hardened their heart, so that they might not look with their eyes, and understand with their heart and turn — and I would heal them." Isaiah said this because he saw his glory and spoke about him. Nevertheless many, even of the authorities, believed in him. But because of the Pharisees they did not confess it, for fear that they would be put out of the synagogue; for they loved human glory more than the glory that comes from God.

COMMENTARY

That Jesus didn't skip to the crucifixion, as though it were some afternoon duty to do and then his work would be done, is a comfort to all of us who struggle with our faithfulness. If Jesus' soul was troubled, how much more should ours be also, when called upon to suffer.

The heavenly voice of comfort, however, was not just for him, but also for us. We are the ones who need the voices and the signs the most, before committing ourselves to the Light. Christ committed himself before the voice. In a sense, that commitment ("Father, glorify your name") was the beginning of the end (the crucifixion), and the beginning of the beginning (the resurrection).

We, in our weakness, need more evidence. Yet in the end, evidence always fails, for there is always another way to explain a voice or a miracle. In the end, it comes to grace through faith, nothing more and nothing less.

PRAYER 44

Lord, your soul was troubled, but you had no need to hear the Father's voice. You dreaded the dying and the pain, but you had no doubt that you were doing the Father's will. That you never looked back, to what "might have been" if you had stayed to minister as Jesus of Nazareth, shows the singleness of your devotion. You are the true Son, devoted to the Father's plan to save all who look upon you with love.

Lord, we identify so much with the authorities who believed but didn't want to make too much noise about it. Like them, the glory of this world is alluring and doesn't seem so wicked when it is offered. Lots of us try to keep a heavy foot on earth and step toward heaven gingerly with the other. What a sight we must be to you — off balance, but looking pious! Truly, not many of us lean heavily upon you. We want to be able to right ourselves without you. We like a balanced life — balanced everything.

You will not "balance" us, will you, if it means equal portions of you and the world? We strive for a balance that is no balance at all. It is not confidence in you, but stability of purpose and safety that we desire. It is wanting you somewhat, but not totally. We do like our options, Lord! We like your light, but we have difficulty believing in it even while we're walking in it. We keep looking for a brighter light, a more pleasant light, a romantic light, an exciting light. We want to be dazzled, Lord, not led. We want to have our senses awed, our minds blinded, our fun continuous. We look at your light out of the corner of our eyes and try to keep the Way in view, without centering our steps upon it. We like walking next to the path, but not on it.

Lord, you hid yourself from them. You were no longer willing to shine on their way from a skewed position. No longer were you willing to be an indirect light.

Lord, we are just like one of the authorities. We want to believe in you, but secretly. We don't want it to interfere with our day, much less our lives, and we certainly don't want to risk our well-being among the world's people, people you've placed in our lives to love. We know how clever that sentence is, Lord. You don't have to remind us. We know we are only trying to justify our lack of public enthusiasm for you. How quickly you show us our mixed devotion, our hiding of a clear, manifest faith behind a supposed love for others.

Lord, you hid yourself from them, and now we suppose you have hidden yourself from us, because we are so much in the world. You have hidden yourself from the church that wants both your glory and the glory of the world. You ask for more than we can give on our own, Lord. You ask us to want you above all else. You ask us to have eyes only for you. You ask us to walk only in one light, your light.

You hid yourself from them, Lord. We can't get over it. You wouldn't let them see you. You peeked out from behind whatever and watched them walk in darkness.

Lord, show us your path, and give us the courage to walk it. Do not forsake us, Lord, else our fall will be forever. Take our hand, and when we will not extend it, reach into our pockets and pull it out. Take our hands, and when we try to pull away, grip us tighter. Take our hands, Lord, we cannot see without you. Take our hands, Lord, now. Amen.

45. GIFT FROM THE FATHER

John 12:44-50

Then Jesus cried aloud: "Whoever believes in me believes not in me but in him who sent me. And whoever sees me sees him who sent me. I have come as light into the world, so that everyone who believes in me should not remain in the darkness. I do not judge anyone who hears my words and does not keep them, for I came not to judge the world, but to save the world. The one who rejects me and does not receive my word has a judge; on the last day the word that I have spoken will serve as judge, for I have not spoken on my own, but the Father who sent me has himself given me a commandment about what to say and what to speak. And I know that his commandment is eternal life. What I speak, therefore, I speak just as the Father has told me."

COMMENTARY

Jesus is pointing to the Father again, as the One who is behind every word and action of his own. He is under orders, as we would understand it in military terms, to do duty. He is, however, not working blindly as many are called upon to do who serve their country. He has been told the mission, he has agreed to its terms, and he is obedient in every way to the Heavenly Father, who loves us like an only begotten child.

It is not only Jesus who loves us. The Heavenly Father loves us equally. Three times in this short passage Jesus refers to the Heavenly Father as he "who sent me." We do not have a Heavenly Father who has to be placated or appeased. The whole Godhead, Father, Son, and Holy Spirit, is on our side, wooing us with love, directing us with the Light of Jesus the Christ.

PRAYER 45

Lord Jesus, Sent One, how much you love the Father. Lord Jesus, Sent One, how much you love us, too. You came to us willingly sent, but sent nonetheless. You came to us as Light, and not to judge. You came to speak the Word, and that Word is eternal life, a gift from the loving Heavenly Father.

You say that there is no catch, no thing we can do, no prayer we can make, no way we can be saved, unless you do it. You will not let us help. You will not let us take any pride in our salvation. It is your gift. It can come to us in no other way.

Such grace, Lord, is too much for us sometimes. We want to help you help us. We want to be saved because we've got it coming. We want to get salvation honorably: we want to earn it.

Lord, salvation is too big a thing for us to help with. Overcoming death and the devil is too big for our little hearts and wills. It is something only you can accomplish, something you must give, and we must receive without merit, else it cannot work its mystery and majesty. It is all so humbling to us, Lord. Yet you don't ask us to crawl to the throne of grace. You come to us instead.

Lord, so often when you've come to us we have looked the other way. You have been sent so frequently to us, by the Heavenly Father, that we have come to expect all our good fortune as due us. You have come, on occasion, clearly enough to overwhelm us with your presence, yet we let the memory fade, and the doubts return, and we wonder if it was really you.

Our enemy, Lord, is constantly after us. Our enemy, Lord, fills our minds with doubt and indecision. He scoffs at us and our little faiths and tells us that you have much more important things to do than work with us. He tells us that you are very busy, far away, invisible, and mean. He tells us that you will not be there at the end of our time, and that our minds are filled with wishful thinking.

You were sent, Lord Jesus Christ! You were sent. You were sent, and you came, and you told us that you are among us as one of us. You came as the light of the world. You came to serve, and in that serving you showed us what God is like. You came for the sake of eternal life so we wouldn't be too worried about the future. You came to win us with love. Amen.

46. LORD OF THE WASHBASIN

John 13:1-20

Now before the festival of the Passover, Jesus knew that his hour had come to depart from this world and go to the Father. Having loved his own who were in the world, he loved them to the end. The devil had already put it into the heart of Judas son of Simon Iscariot to betray him. And during supper Jesus, knowing that the Father had given all things into his hands, and that he had come from God and was going to God, got up from the table, took off his outer robe, and tied a towel around himself. Then he poured water into a basin and began to wash the disciples' feet and to wipe them with the towel that was tied around him. He came to Simon Peter, who said to him, "Lord, are you going to wash my feet?" Jesus answered, "You do not know now what I am doing, but later you will understand." Peter said to him, "You will never wash my feet." Jesus answered, "Unless I wash you, you have no share with me." Simon Peter said to him, "Lord, not my feet only but also my hands and my head!" Jesus said to him, "One who has bathed does not need to wash, except for the feet, but is entirely clean. And you are clean, though not all of you." For he knew who was to betray him; for this reason he said, "Not all of you are clean."

After he had washed their feet, had put on his robe, and had returned to the table, he said to them, "Do you know what I have done to you? You call me Teacher and Lord — and you are right, for that is what I am. So if I, your Lord and Teacher, have washed your feet, you also ought to wash one another's feet. For I have set you an example, that you also should do as I have done to you. Very truly, I tell you, servants are not greater than their master, nor are messengers greater than the one who sent them. If you know these things, you are blessed if you do them. I am not speaking of all of you; I know whom I have chosen. But it is to fulfill the scripture, 'The one who ate my bread has lifted his heel against me.' I tell you this now, before it occurs, so that when it does occur, you may believe that I am he. Very truly, I tell you, whoever receives one whom I send receives me; and whoever receives me receives him who sent me."

COMMENTARY

The washing of the disciples' feet by Jesus is an example to us to serve one another, and proof that he really did love his disciples to the end, as Jesus clearly explains. However, it is also an act of such personal humility by Christ that none of us could duplicate it, no matter how many other people's feet we would wash. No one is as beneath us as we are beneath Christ. If we were to wash our greatest enemy's feet in love, even this would not approach Christ's act. Nevertheless, this is what we are told to do, and the church has largely interpreted these words symbolically.

This passage contains the first use of the word "messenger" in the Gospel of John. It is applied by Christ, not only as a reference to him and what he has been, but also what he expects us to be.

PRAYER 46

Lord Jesus Christ, we identify with Peter. He knew that it was "not right" for you to be doing this to him. He knew that the roles had gotten reversed. He knew that he was not worthy to have this happen to him from you.

Also, Lord, we identify with nearly all the Christian world that has let this mandate to "wash one another's feet" become so symbolic that the practice is almost nonexistent. Yet we know that you expect us to do this in more than symbolic ways. You expect us to care for one another, making no one our inferior.

Lord, we can hardly imagine you kneeling before us. All our lives we have knelt before you and the Father in a posture of devotion. We can more easily imagine you dying on the cross for us than kneeling before us, washbasin and towel in hand. After all, if you are dying for us, you are boldly taking on our great enemies of sin, death, and the devil. But if you are washing our feet, you are singling us out for love. You are being so personal, so tender, so momentous, that we can never forget the touch, the act, the look on your face beneath us. Lord, we can't stand to think of it, even now.

Is it because we know that if we let you do this to us, we must also do it to others who we feel are beneath us? If we let you do this to us, must we have you haunting us, all the days of our lives, not only as the Lord of the cross, but of the washbasin as well? My feet warm just thinking about it.

What kind of God are you, Lord, to wash the feet of followers like us? No wonder the world doesn't follow you. And we must wonder if we are following also, with this monstrous reluctance to have you touch us as you touched Peter. Do we want you that intimate with us?

We want to cry out with Peter, "Yes, Lord, do it to me now." But our heart is far from our head in this matter. We think we would rather wash another's feet than have you wash ours. We think we could be more in control of the matter that way.

Lord Jesus Christ, follow us all the days of our lives, until we say, "Yes, Lord, do it now." Do not let us run from you forever. Hound us with washbasin and towel, until we are clean, until we are yours. Until then, we will not know what it means to be all yours. Amen.

47. LOVE AND DIFFICULT TIMES

John 13:21-35

After saying this Jesus was troubled in spirit, and declared, "Very truly, I tell you, one of you will betray me." The disciples looked at one another, uncertain of whom he was speaking. One of his disciples — the one whom Jesus loved — was reclining next to him; Simon Peter therefore motioned to him to ask Jesus of whom he was speaking. So while reclining next to Jesus, he asked him, "Lord, who is it?" Jesus answered, "It is the one to whom I give this piece of bread when I have dipped it in the dish." So when he had dipped the piece of bread, he gave it to Judas son of Simon Iscariot. After he received the piece of bread, Satan entered into him. Jesus said to him, "Do quickly what you are going to do." Now no one at the table knew why he said this to him. Some thought that, because Judas had the common purse, Jesus was telling him, "Buy what we need for the festival"; or, that he should give something to the poor. So, after receiving the piece of bread, he immediately went out. And it was night.

When he had gone out, Jesus said, "Now the Son of Man has been glorified, and God has been glorified in him. If God has been glorified in him, God will also glorify him in himself and will glorify him at once. Little children, I am with you only a little longer. You will look for me; and as I said to the Jews so now I say to you, 'Where I am going, you cannot come.' I give you a new commandment, that you love one another. Just as I have loved you, you also should love one another. By this everyone will know that you are my disciples, if you have love for one another."

COMMENTARY

Betrayal is a bitter enough experience, but foreknowledge of that betrayal, where one's death will be forfeited because of it, must be excruciatingly sorrowful. Obviously, Jesus could have stopped Judas, but he didn't. Instead, that same night, he gave the great mandate, the great command, which Maundy Thursday has recalled through the centuries: love one another, as I have loved you.

It is important to note that this command was not given in a moment of gushing, rushing sentimentality, but on the night of betrayal. It contains, therefore, much more than an emotional urge. It is the way to live, and the way to die.

PRAYER 47

Lord Jesus, we are great lovers when we sense that "God's in his heaven — all's right with the world!" We can really love when being loved. We can be so nice when everything is going right for us, which is, thanks to you, most of the time. But sometimes, Lord, people are difficult, friends are scarce, danger abounds for us or one we love, or betrayal is in the air. Sometimes, Lord, loving doesn't seem to be the right thing to be doing.

To care for another, more than our own predicament, is tough love, Lord. To really worry about someone else more than ourselves is too demanding a love. Lord, we like gentle love, tender words, nice people, good times. Tell us to love one another on a starlit night, when the music's been fine, the food terrific, the company superb. Tell us to love when our healthy kids are tucked in bed, our parents are understanding, our promotion has been accomplished, our new thing paid for in full. Lord, don't tell us to love one another on the night of your betrayal. Look what you do to love! You take all the romance out of it. You take love out of the world of dreams and fantasy and tell us to love under the most difficult of times. Who do you think we are? How could we ever do that?

Without you, Lord, we cannot love like you. None of us can. We know what makes us happy, and when we are happy, then we can love! That makes sense. But you tell us to love, regardless of our predicament. You tell us to love, no matter what our difficulty or crisis may be. You mandate it. You Maundy Thursday it. You put it all in the context of great pain and sorrow, on the threshold of betrayal and death, and say, "Now, love."

Lord, who knows what love is under such circumstances? Who has a spirit like yours to see clearly how to do it? How much endurance do you think we have? And, truthfully now, what good will loving like that do us?

Lord, in the asking of the question, we know we are missing the point of loving. We are trying to do it for ourselves again, for our own benefit. You won't let love work that way, though we want it to. Love is for you and for someone else. You desire that we do it without a thought of deriving a benefit for ourselves. You crave to see it being done by us. You delight in seeing us beyond ourselves, letting love occur at the most impossible times. You know it is the power beyond all other powers, your power, overcoming the world. You know that we have seldom done it, if ever. You keep urging us on, showing us your example, reminding us of your words, saying, do it, do it, do it.

You did it, Lord, on the night of your betrayal. You let love. You did what you commanded us to do. When we are under stress, Lord, unable to love, remind us of that dark night when you shone so brightly. Remind us of what you said, and what you did, and who you did it for ... for the Father, and for us. Thank you, loving Lord. Amen.

48. WINNING US BACK

John 13:36-38

Simon Peter said to him, "Lord, where are you going?" Jesus answered, "Where I am going, you cannot follow me now; but you will follow afterward." Peter said to him, "Lord, why can I not follow you now? I will lay down my life for you." Jesus answered, "Will you lay down your life for me? Very truly, I tell you, before the cock crows, you will have denied me three times."

COMMENTARY

Our heartfelt commitment to Christ is such a fragile thing. Though Peter doubtlessly believed he was ready to die for Christ, Christ knew how much Peter was still in this world.

PRAYER 48

Lord Jesus Christ, if you had given Peter a word of encouragement, perhaps he would have been strengthened to serve you. Had you shown some confidence in him, perhaps he would have remembered it when his moment came to tell the truth about his discipleship. That's how we want you to deal with us; buoy us up, inspire us, cheer us on with bravado, but don't speak harsh words of our pending denial of you. It's hard enough to believe in you without your telling us that we are weak.

Yes, we are weak, Lord. We know it without being told. We know that we cannot begin to accomplish what we wish we could do for you. Your way isn't all that clear in a world with so much cynicism, so much need for self-pleasure. And showing too much attention to you and your words gets us labeled real fast. You don't need any more fanatics.

Yet, Lord, in your words to Peter there is hope. You tell Peter that he can follow you later. You tell him that there will be a time when he can join you, wherever it is you are going. You tell him that he won't be lost, despite his denial. You tell him that much history has to occur before you're together again, and forever, but that it will come.

Lord, that news had to comfort him, had to be in his mind for the rest of his days. That news, if he could remember it, just had to make all the struggling worthwhile. Say the same words to us, Lord, even though none of us really wants to suffer as Peter did.

Where were you going, Lord, when you told Peter he couldn't follow yet? Were you going back home to the Father? Were you going to the cross to die the most beautiful death? Were you going some other place for some other reason?

It seems as though you were speaking about your dying, and being able to do it with love in your heart for others, despite its cruelty. It seems as though you were telling Peter that someday he could die like you, filled with compassion for the world, unafraid for the future. It seems as though you were telling him that you had to do it first, in order to show him the way.

Lord Jesus Christ, first back from the grave, lead us into the next life with every confidence that even if we, like Peter, were to deny you before the end, you would be there for us, winning us back. Do not give up on us, O Lord. Do not give up on us, any more than you gave up on Peter. Amen.

49. ENJOY THE FATHER

John 14:1-7

"Do not let your hearts be troubled. Believe in God, believe also in me. In my Father's house there are many dwelling places. If it were not so, would I have told you that I go to prepare a place for you? And if I go and prepare a place for you, I will come again and will take you to myself, so that where I am, there you may be also. And you know the way to the place where I am going." Thomas said to him, "Lord, we do not know where you are going. How can we know the way?" Jesus said to him, "I am the way, and the truth, and the life. No one comes to the Father except through me. If you know me, you will know my Father also. From now on you do know him and have seen him."

COMMENTARY

This is another one of the seven "I am" sayings of Jesus in the Gospel of John. However, Jesus not only tells us who he is (the way, the truth, and the life), but also where he is going (to the Father), and what he's going to do when he gets there (prepare a place for us, in order that we can be together again). The only access to the Father is through Jesus the Christ.

PRAYER 49

Lord Jesus, you tell us that you are the "way," which implies that there is some place to travel toward. You make it clear that that some*place* is a some*one*, the Heavenly Father. You are the only route, the only means, to the Father. How much you must love the Father. How much you yearn for us to know him as you do. How anxious you are for us to be with you in the place called "Father's house."

Lord, it is hard for us to imagine a place you've been busy preparing for two millennia. With all your creative power, it seems as though it would be done by now! We know, Lord, that you are beyond this kind of logic. You do not think in mere mortal terms of years and time.

What you seem to be saying is, "You've just got to meet the Heavenly Father. He is unlike anyone you've ever met, beyond the weaknesses and frailties of our earthly parents." Your love is showing, Lord, when you talk about the Father. You make us wonder how completely different God is from any of us. You make us see how important it is to know that you are the way to the only God of love.

Lord, you also tell us that you are the "truth." Sometimes truth seems to be the most important thing in this world of discernment. There are so many sides to every issue. Nothing is simple. We become fatigued with the complexity of it all. Yet you claim to be "the" truth. What can you mean but that you are the only reality, the one authentic person ever to live in human form, the only human being ever to have direct access to God, because you were sent from God on a mission to claim us? That is the "truth" about you. You have said it over and over. You keep telling us why you came, and why you come to be among us. You want us to enjoy the Father as you do. That is the truth.

Lord Jesus Christ, you tell us that you are the "life," which must mean that you are, by example and presence, the only way really to enjoy this earth-time experience. You are the only way to live it up right. You alone know how to savor every moment without losing sight of what is yet to come. Living life your way is living with both feet on earth, doing the deeds that are uniquely ours to do, and enjoying the people you place in our lives, without forgetting that our hearts beat in the loving heart of the Heavenly Father.

Lord Jesus, forgive us if we get sidetracked with earthly notions of fatherhood when thinking about the Heavenly Father. Forgive all of us who are fathers and mothers who have distorted the perfect image of divine parenthood. Forgive us when we use our own experience with less than perfect parents as a limitation of your grace for us. Help us all come to call your Father "our Father," with the same sort of energy and love you expressed as the way, the truth, and the life. Amen.

50. LEAVING QUESTIONS BEHIND

John 14:8-14

Philip said to him, "Lord, show us the Father, and we will be satisfied." Jesus said to him, "Have I been with you all this time, Philip, and you still do not know me? Whoever has seen me has seen the Father. How can you say, 'Show us the Father?' Do you not believe that I am in the Father and the Father is in me? The words that I say to you I do not speak on my own; but the Father who dwells in me does his works. Believe me that I am in the Father and the Father is in me; but if you do not, then believe me because of the works themselves. Very truly, I tell you, the one who believes in me will also do the works that I do, and, in fact, will do greater works than these, because I am going to the Father. I will do whatever you ask in my name, so that the Father may be glorified in the Son. If in my name you ask me for anything, I will do it."

COMMENTARY

Philip's question struck a raw nerve in Jesus. Having just said that he and the Father were one, and that he was the way to the Father, Philip dares suggest: "Lord, show us the Father, and we will be satisfied." The inclusion of Philip's name in Jesus' answer (like a parent scolding a child) indicates the profound disappointment Jesus is expressing. However, the additional statements Jesus makes are so profound that they require much more prayer than this one alone.

PRAYER 50

Lord, now you are way over our heads. Now you make promises to us that we don't know how to interpret. It is possible for us to imagine that you and the Father are one. We can believe that the Father speaks through you, as you say. We believe that the Father is in you and that you are in the Father, but, Lord, we aren't doing the works you did, and we are not asking for much in your name, expecting you to do it.

Where has the power gone, Lord? Where has our faith gone? If we say that we fail to do the great things you did, because our faith is weak, we are saying that strong faith does miracles, not you. If we say that we are not asking rightly, then it's a "procedure" or "technique" that seems to be the key to win your support and power. If we say we will clean up our wicked lives so you can use them for your glory, we are vainly trying to save ourselves by good works. Yet if you clean up our lives, through the miracle of forgiveness, we are clean indeed, and the block to your power should be gone. But it isn't.

Lord, we have little difficulty understanding that you can do all things, but whether or not you do powerful things through us is not so clear. We see miraculous cures every day, through the gift of medicine you've given to us. We see people brought back from the brink of death, again and again, through science. We see people run for safety from predicted hurricanes and other natural disasters, because you have let us learn earth's ways. We see agents of mercy in the most horrendous of situations and wonder if that is you at work. We use all sorts of new ways to reduce hunger through high-yield crops, and we wonder if that is you. If so, it is glorious.

We see the other side, too, Lord. We see disputes settled violently, bombs burning babies, and the sword being a delight to the eyes of many. We see the homeless without shelter, the hungry with potbellied stomachs, and most of the world with less than it needs for dignified living. We are overwhelmed with the horror of it all.

What can we say, Lord? You give us the way, but we go astray. You give us the truth, but we confuse it. You give us the life, and we waste it. All true, but where is your promised power? Where are the supernatural signs for us to see that we might believe? How do you expect us to understand these magnanimous promises of yours, if the power is delivered through natural means only?

Lord God, Jesus the Christ, we leave these questions at your throne, trusting that you will guide some among us to be vehicles of your own grace, in ways we will never understand. We leave these doubts behind, trusting that you are about your Father's business with us, and that we are accomplishing more than we know. We let go of our hungry need for displays of power, and trust that your will is being done, on earth as it is in heaven.

As we leave these things behind, Lord, keep us mindful that the moment might come, at any time, to be your agent of healing, your agent of reconciliation, your agent of love and friendship. Keep us mindful, Lord. Keep us hopeful and alert. And when your power does course through us to another for your love's sake, give us the greatest power of all, to recognize that it was you in us doing the Father's will. Amen.

51. COVERED

John 14:15-24

"If you love me, you will keep my commandments. And I will ask the Father, and he will give you another Advocate, to be with you forever. This is the Spirit of truth, whom the world cannot receive, because it neither sees him nor knows him. You know him, because he abides with you, and he will be in you.

"I will not leave you orphaned; I am coming to you. In a little while the world will no longer see me, but you will see me; because I live, you also will live. On that day you will know that I am in my Father, and you in me, and I in you. They who have my commandments and keep them are those who love me; and those who love me will be loved by my Father, and I will love them and reveal myself to them." Judas (not Iscariot) said to him, "Lord, how is it that you will reveal yourself to us, and not to the world?" Jesus answered him, "Those who love me will keep my word, and my Father will love them, and we will come to them and make our home with them. Whoever does not love me does not keep my words; and the word that you hear is not mine, but is from the Father who sent me."

COMMENTARY

Jesus is taking care of our loneliness in this passage. He knows that we will need his presence in a special way, so the Advocate is named as his Spirit of truth. He knows that we will feel like orphans living in the wrong world, so he promises to come and live with us. He offers, at last, the greatest possible company for those who love him: the Father, with the Son, "making home" with us.

PRAYER 51

Lord Jesus, you know how important your physical coming to us has been. You walked this earth as one of us. You slept here, played here, worked here, and loved here. In the body you did these things, and we could see you, hear you, touch you, and talk with you. You were real. You were truth incarnate, truth with a body.

Now you tell us that another Advocate will come to us, a second Advocate. You tell us that the world won't be able to *see* this Advocate, as it could see you, but we will *see* this Spirit of truth because this Advocate will live within us. You tell us that the Father, who loves you and us, will send the Advocate to us out of love.

Lord, we know what authentic Advocates are and what they do. We know that they are real, not imaginary. You are promising to defend us, in a *real* way, promising to stand in the way of those who would harm us, and to speak well of us in a world that has very tiny ears for things of the spirit. You are promising to encourage us, to be here with us with comfort when we need it, and to prod us when we get lazy. You are promising your presence, the Advocate's presence, and the Father's presence. You promise not only to be within us, but also to surround us. You are telling us that we need not despair, even when we feel lonely, for you've got us covered.

As Advocate, Lord, you are promising to advise us, to let us know your way, and you are promising *really* to do this, not just figuratively, not just through our imaginations. You tell us that we will be able to see what the world cannot see, namely, your company.

You didn't tell lone individuals about the Advocate, Lord. You told it to them together. You were placing us, even then, into companies of believers, squadrons of the faithful. You didn't tell us that "individual audiences" were all we would ever need. Instead, you promised to be with us, in the plural, as Advocate.

Lord Jesus, we usually prefer you solo, one on one. Other people distract us when we pray. We like to have you all to ourselves. Others interfere with our concentration, our imagination. But when it's an urgent need, Lord, it's usually through other human beings like ourselves that you come. You send us out of our closets and away from our musings so that real helpers in physical form can aid us. You send us an example we can see, an advocate to counsel us, a champion who is strong when we are weak, a person with gifts we need but do not have at that moment.

Lord, your way is marvelously dependent upon the communion of saints. What we would privatize, you make public. What we would selfishly personalize, you brandish among the faithful. What we would hold preciously close, like a child with a teddy bear, you take away, so that we can see how much more you have to give through others than we could possibly ever hold on our own.

Lord Jesus, use us as your advocates. Let us be your presence to others. Use whatever special gifts you have given to us. Give us the eyes of the gathered faithful that see you in myriad ministries for the sake of one another. And, Lord Advocate, give us the wisdom not only to thank the faithful, but also to thank you for using us among them. Amen.

52. A GREATER SACRIFICE

John 14:25-31
"I have said these things to you while I am still with you. But the Advocate, the Holy Spirit, whom the Father will send in my name, will teach you everything, and remind you of all that I have said to you. Peace I leave with you; my peace I give to you. I do not give to you as the world gives. Do not let your hearts be troubled, and do not let them be afraid. You heard me say to you, 'I am going away, and I am coming to you.' If you loved me, you would rejoice that I am going to the Father, because the Father is greater than I. And now I have told you this before it occurs, so that when it does occur, you may believe. I will no longer talk much with you, for the ruler of this world is coming. He has no power over me; but I do as the Father has commanded me, so that the world may know that I love the Father. Rise, let us be on our way."

COMMENTARY

The peace that comes from God is given. It cannot be attained in any other way. This is one of the distinctive characteristics of God's peace. It cannot be earned or seized. It is a gift. The fearful or troubled heart is a heart in need of a gift, not a task. It's a heart that needs to be opened, not burdened with guilt or duty. Peace, as given by Christ, is his accomplishment in us, not our attainment of him.

Jesus was in the flesh when he spoke: "The Father is greater than I." All that Jesus does he does to convince the world, not the Father, that he loves the Father beyond all else, and bids us do the same. After the resurrection, full unity with the Father was restored, and there is no recognized superiority of one person of the Trinity over another.

PRAYER 52

Peace, Lord, you promise to give *peace*. You tell us not to be afraid, not to be upset, yet we wallow in fear every day. Our imaginations tell us to be afraid. They create monster scenarios for ourselves and for those we love. Our imaginations conjure up devastation upon devastation, and we are robbed of peace.

Lord, what shall we do with such vivid fear? Sometimes our prayers become pleas for deliverance from foes that don't even exist, except in our minds. Our days are spent insuring against all kinds of disaster. We walk like a wounded animal being hounded. We wonder when the terror moment will come to us. We have no confidence in this world of woes.

When you talk about "peace," Lord, you are talking about going to the Father. When you promise to give peace, you make it clear that it's different from the world's peace. You have your eyes in another realm, your ears tuned to another's voice, your heart in the embrace of a Father more loving than imagination can create.

Lord, you want the world to know you love the Father. Why do you want the world to know this? More than anyone else, you alone have targeted the Father for love. Why does it matter if we know it, unless you want us to follow your example to peace? You don't escape into melancholy thoughts about the beauty of the day or the beauty of the place. You simply know there is a Father worth loving beyond all else, a Father in heaven whose name is holy, a Father who sent you to us to tell us all about him.

Lord, when I think of you, I am not afraid. When I think of your yearning for the Father, my heart is joyful. When I think of our Father, I think of him who gave more than his life by giving you up. His sacrifice of you, Jesus, is even greater than the sacrifice of himself. You he loved beyond all others. You he would protect from every harm. For you he would lay down his own life, if only he could. He would do anything to spare you, but he could not do this without losing us, his other beloved children. Neither he nor you could stop it, Lord, else the sacrifice would be lessened, and we would be lost forever.

We cannot attain this love, Lord. It is too high. We cannot do it. We can more easily give up our own lives to sacrifice than those whom you've given to us as beloved family. Only our heavenly Father, who filled you with peace at approaching death, can do it. Only the Father, whom you knew so well, could take away your fear of the cross. Amen.

53. FOR THE SAKE OF FRUIT

John 15:1-11

"I am the true vine, and my Father is the vinegrower. He removes every branch in me that bears no fruit. Every branch that bears fruit he prunes to make it bear more fruit. You have already been cleansed by the word that I have spoken to you. Abide in me as I abide in you. Just as the branch cannot bear fruit by itself unless it abides in the vine, neither can you unless you abide in me. I am the vine, you are the branches. Those who abide in me and I in them bear much fruit, because apart from me you can do nothing. Whoever does not abide in me is thrown away like a branch and withers; such branches are gathered, thrown into the fire, and burned. If you abide in me, and my words abide in you, ask for whatever you wish, and it will be done for you. My Father is glorified by this, that you bear much fruit and become my disciples. As the Father has loved me, so I have loved you; abide in my love. If you keep my commandments, you will abide in my love, just as I have kept my Father's commandments and abide in his love. I have said these things to you so that my joy may be in you, and that your joy may be complete."

COMMENTARY

This lesson is about vines and branches, bearing fruit, asking for God's help, and completed joy. It is also about pruning, judgment, warning, and fire. There are promises and warnings, fruit and fire. The vine, Jesus Christ, is the key to productive life and love. Unless our branch is anchored in him, there is no life force capable of producing fruit.

PRAYER 53

Lord, we cannot escape your pruning shears. Whether we do good or bad, the sharp cut of your knife always seems poised at our throats. You do not let our lives go to leaf. It hurts, Lord, when you prune. We bleed as certainly as a spring cut twig. It hurts, Lord, and it is hard not to fear that you may overcut us, thereby killing us. It is hard to remember that what you are doing to us, you do *for* us, and for the sake of fruit.

Sometimes, Lord, we wonder about your pruning technique. We know, partially, what effect you have on us when you cut out of our lives someone we've thought very precious. Our investment in the resurrection grows substantially! But, Lord, when it grows this way, we worry about our motives for wanting the new life to come. Sometimes it feels more like yearning for reunion with those we've loved and lost, than union with you for all time.

We cannot know, Lord, about the lost loved ones, and how you justify it to them. All we can see is your pruning from this side of eternal life. When you take one of us away, especially prematurely, what are we to think of his loss of this life's experience? How are we to justify it? How do you justify it? Surely there is more to it than making fruit come from us who remain.

Lord, you know what we're hinting at. You know your way appears cruel to the survivor. You know that our questions are endless about the "why." We never get a satisfactory answer. You keep telling us that it will become clear later, to have faith, to wait. You make us all feel so expendable. For the sake of fruit would you sacrifice any one of us?

How you love the unbelievers, Lord. You are forever giving them examples of your faithful people not giving up on you nor giving in to despair. How you wish to bring them into the family of faith. You will let us bear any indignity for their sakes, and they don't even know it. You count us as sheep for the slaughter, hoping that one of them will see your supportive love reflected in us. It is a hard task, Lord. It is a heavy yoke. You use us and expect us not to complain too bitterly about it. How can you expect us to love the unbelieving world this much? We are not you!

Lord, if it were left up to us, we would have called it quits long ago with the faithless world. We would declare it a lost cause. We would do that, except we remember that once we were a part of the world of unbelief. Were it not for the memory of a time in our lives without you, we would not see any purpose for your waiting to end it all.

Thank you for waiting for us, Lord. Thank you for not giving up too quickly on the world and us. Thank you for pruning those persons who have touched us more deeply than they know, because we see your love in them. Thank you for the hope of being pruned by you for your kingdom's sake. Amen.

54. FRIENDS

John 15:12-17
"This is my commandment, that you love one another as I have loved you. No one has greater love than this, to lay down one's life for one's friends. You are my friends if you do what I command you. I do not call you servants any longer, because the servant does not know what the master is doing; but I have called you friends, because I have made known to you everything that I have heard from my Father. You did not choose me but I chose you. And I appointed you to go and bear fruit, fruit that will last, so that the Father will give you whatever you ask him in my name. I am giving you these commands so that you may love one another."

COMMENTARY

The church has preferred the servant passages of Scripture over this one of being "friend" to Jesus. It is far easier to be a servant than a friend. A servant only has to do the bidding of the master. A friend has to care, has to love, *and* do the bidding of the master.

As friends of God, we are called to a higher calling than servants of God. As friends, we have no time off, no limits to our task, no hesitancy to be wherever God wants us. As friends, we are partners with God, "in on" his work and purpose, and not mere pawns to do his will.

PRAYER 54

Lord God, who among us can know you or your ways? You are known to us as the hidden God, beyond us, like infinity, too big to grasp, too deep to understand. You are engaged in cosmic battles against principalities and powers, the size and nature of which no poet has been able to express, no mortal able to imagine without devastating fear and trembling. You, Lord, creator of worlds beyond us, can hardly call us "friend," for we, in comparison to all that you have made, must be as nothing. We must be as expendable as dust, of no more value than a passing thought. It is hard to believe that we are important to you. That contradicts logic, science, and common sense.

You call us "friends" as though we were allies and companions. You call us friends as though we could really care about one another, as though you would accept love from us, as well as give us love. By calling us "friend" you link up with us and take our side. Lord, we can hardly make friends with each other as mortals; how do you expect us to make friends with you, the immortal one?

Because you call us "friend" you say that you have let us in on you and what you are doing. You picked us out from all the creatures you have made, yet we hardly know you ourselves. We are the blind leading the blind. We didn't choose you. You chose us. You said so yourself. And now you want us to bear fruit for you, and that can only mean that you want us to find some new friends for you to love along with us.

Lord, what is "the fruit that will last," unless it is intimate knowledge of you as our friend? It can't be anything less. It must be knowing what to ask of you, as a friend would ask of a friend. It must not be using you. No true friend would use another friend. It must be trusting you with our innermost thoughts and secrets, our fears and our hopes, our failures and shortcomings, our loves and our loved ones.

Lord, friends share with one another. If it's a real friendship, it's not a one-way friendship. When we reflect upon what you've shared about yourself with us, it is very personal. We've heard you praying in secret, only because you told us what you said. We heard you weeping when Lazarus died, because you loved him. We heard you tell us how heavy your soul was on the night of your betrayal. We heard you wonder aloud if we would all go off and leave you, when your teachings got tough. We heard you tell us again how wonderful the Father is, and how we should rejoice that you are going to him. We heard you say that you are here to lose nothing, but to raise it all up on the last day. What a friend you have been, though we didn't know what to do but listen.

Lord Jesus Christ, you have been a friend. You crumble the walls of logic with love. You won't let rational doubt win the argument that you are too big to care about us. With a kiss, with friendship, with sharing, you penetrate our hearts, and no amount of thinking about it makes sense. As we invite our friends to meet you, may they be "the fruit" that endures forever, raised up on the last day, according to your purpose and promise. Amen.

55. HARDSHIP AS SERVICE

John 15:18—16:4a

"If the world hates you, be aware that it hated me before it hated you. If you belonged to the world, the world would love you as its own. Because you do not belong to the world, but I have chosen you out of the world — therefore the world hates you. Remember the word that I said to you, 'Servants are not greater than their master.' If they persecuted me, they will persecute you; if they kept my word, they will keep yours also. But they will do all these things to you on account of my name, because they do not know him who sent me. If I had not come and spoken to them, they would not have sin; but now they have no excuse for their sin. Whoever hates me hates my Father also. If I had not done among them the works that no one else did, they would not have sin. But now they have seen and hated both me and my Father. It was to fulfill the word that is written in their law, 'They hated me without a cause.'

"When the Advocate comes, whom I will send to you from the Father, the spirit of truth who comes from the Father, he will testify on my behalf. You also are to testify because you have been with me from the beginning.

"I have said these things to you to keep you from stumbling. They will put you out of the synagogues. Indeed, an hour is coming when those who kill you will think that by doing so they are offering worship to God. And they will do this because they have not known the Father or me. But I have said these things to you so that when their hour comes you may remember that I told you about them."

COMMENTARY

It is easy to suppose from this text that we ought to expect the world to hate us, and if it doesn't, to do something offensive enough to make sure that it happens. Christ doesn't ask us to make the world hate us, but rather, not to be surprised if it happens. Persecution, like suffering, is not something necessary to bring upon oneself. It comes, and it comes without cause.

When the hour of persecution comes, we are neither called upon to resist nor to despair, but to remember that this is to be expected, and that it also happened to the Christ. What is most difficult for us to handle is to receive persecution from the hands of someone committed to God, who believes that the hardship or suffering inflicted upon us is service to the Almighty.

PRAYER 55

Lord, persecution from believers is far more painful than anything the world can dish out to us. We expect the people of the world to resist you and us, but to receive rejection or ridicule or offense from sincere people is like being rejected by one's family. How can you afford to have a divided house? How can you expect us to bear the indignity of pious people's wrath? We are not as strong as you.

Lord, we have all felt exactly what you told us was coming. We know what it's like to be quietly ignored, dismissed as eccentric, labeled as simplistic. We have felt a little of this kind of wrath, and some of us have felt a great deal of this sort of judgment. Not only is the experience disheartening, it fills us with doubt about our own loyalty to you and our own conclusions about how to be your advocate.

In this time, we dare not be intolerant of others, even if they be misguided! We believe in the rights of others, and we have been taught not to force our views on anyone. We respect everyone's personal faith journey and don't want to suggest it's missing the mark. We have personalized the faith to the point where there can be no criticism of it. We are quickly asked, "Who are you to question the content of my faith?"

So, Lord, you are done in by what is perceived as your Spirit. All claim the liberty to formulate their own belief system. We have replaced the teachings of our ancestors with our own musings. We like to think you approve of this because it feels so "spiritual." We use your own words to prove our points of view.

Lord, your word is a sharp double-edged sword. It cuts through our personal theologies like a hot swinging sabre. You slay us with words beyond our feelings. You won't let us wallow in pleasure, but you make us see how radically different you are from self-gratification.

You tell us to forgive, when forgiveness is impossible. You tell us to give, when we think we have already done more than our share. You take away from us that which we hold most dear, and you tell us to love you anyway. You let us suffer and tell us, "I told you so." What kind of God are you? Surely you aren't out to win us with gifts! You don't guarantee protection from the enemy, or comfort in this world. You have made all those things look weak and selfish. You keep telling us that there is more to you than these things.

Lord Jesus Christ, lover of the Father, you are his spirit incarnate. You love like him, and then you tell us to love like you. You offer no prize, no certainty at the end of our time, except yourself with the heavenly Father. Even the resurrection is but a promise. But it is your promise.

Be with us, Lord, as we suffer for you, and with you. Remind us of your words, and fill us with such a measure of your love that no enemy can do more than simply end our lives on earth. Amen.

56. THE SIN OF UNBELIEF

John 16:4b-15

"I did not say these things to you from the beginning, because I was with you. But now I am going to him who sent me; yet none of you asks me, 'Where are you going?' But because I have said these things to you, sorrow has filled your hearts. Nevertheless I tell you the truth: it is to your advantage that I go away, for if I do not go away, the Advocate will not come to you; but if I go, I will send him to you. And when he comes, he will prove the world wrong about sin and righteousness and judgment: about sin, because they do not believe in me; about righteousness, because I am going to the Father and you will see me no longer; about judgment, because the ruler of this world has been condemned.

"I still have many things to say to you, but you cannot bear them now. When the Spirit of truth comes, he will guide you into all the truth; for he will not speak on his own, but will speak whatever he hears, and he will declare to you the things that are to come. He will glorify me, because he will take what is mine and declare it to you. All that the Father has is mine. For this reason I said that he will take what is mine and declare it to you."

COMMENTARY

Sin, righteousness, and judgment, the three matters raised by Jesus with his disciples, are so far removed from our daily concerns that we prefer to push these matters to theologians and say, "Please advise."

Sin is not so much about deeds, as is commonly thought, but about nonbelief in Jesus as the Messiah. Righteousness is not simply goodness, as we like to think, but rather, access to the Father. Judgment, in its severest condemnation, is not against us, but against the ruler of this world, Satan.

PRAYER 56

Lord Jesus, nonbelief does not seem nearly as sinful as bad behavior. There, in one sentence, is our common understanding. No one gets injured if we ignore you, Lord, but if we harm another human being in any way, that is quite noticeable. Jails are made for offenders of this sort, but there is no punishment for the sin of nonbelief. We have come to expect it in one another, and in ourselves. We know each other as sinners in many ways, and the sin of nonbelief in you as Messiah appears well down on the gravity list.

Lord Jesus, you proved your righteousness by going back to the Father. It wasn't the resurrection event that proved it; it was your ascension. You were welcomed back as the only begotten Son, as perfect a Son as before you were sent to us. You came into this horrendously sinful place, this place of nonbelief, and never stopped looking toward and talking to the Father. You are righteous, Lord, because Satan could not woo you away from God, though he used every human temptation known. He brought you face to face with the dead, but not one could stay dead around you. He brought you face to face with Pilate and earthly judgment, but you would not break. When nailed to the cross, he made you feel abandoned by the Father, but you still committed your spirit into the Father's care.

Lord Jesus, you have told us that the ruler of this world has been condemned, but you have not yet eliminated him. We know his power. He knows our weaknesses. Because of him, at times we feel as though you have let us become impatient Jobs, abandoned by you and the Father. You have condemned this evil one, but he still rules us with deceptions. Above all, he still tries to make us not believe in you. Sometimes he succeeds. Sometimes he succeeds very easily.

Lord, belief in you is so costly. You want more out of us than we think you should take. You go right by our goods, our talents, and our time and go after our souls. You want our souls. It scares us, because it looks like you are extracting our personality, our vitality, our essence. You want us to believe the impossible, that Almighty God came to earth with the name of Jesus, and was righteous, and beat the ruler of this world at winning our souls.

Lord, you promised to send us the Spirit of truth. You promised that he would guide us, speaking only what he hears from you about what is yet to come. It is the future, Lord, that concerns us most, yet you are already there, forward in time beyond our understanding.

Win us, Lord Jesus, lest we lose forever. Help us win others to you by word and by deed. Don't give up on any of us, as we fight with the ruler of this world. Remember his power. Remember his craftiness. Remember his ruthlessness. Without you, Lord, we cannot stand, even for a moment, against him. Amen.

57. ALL DOUBTS WILL VANISH

John 16:16-33
"A little while, and you will no longer see me, and again a little while, and you will see me." Then some of his disciples said to one another, "What does he mean by saying to us, 'A little while, and you will no longer see me, and again a little while, and you will see me'; and 'Because I am going to the Father'?" They said, "What does he mean by this 'a little while'? We do not know what he is talking about." Jesus knew that they wanted to ask him, so he said to them, "Are you discussing among yourselves what I meant when I said, 'A little while, and you will no longer see me, and again a little while, and you will see me'? Very truly, I tell you, you will weep and mourn, but the world will rejoice; you will have pain, but your pain will turn into joy. When a woman is in labor, she has pain, because her hour has come. But when her child is born, she no longer remembers the anguish because of the joy of having brought a human being into the world. So you have pain now; but I will see you again, and your hearts will rejoice, and no one will take your joy from you. On that day you will ask nothing of me. Very truly, I tell you, if you ask anything of the Father in my name; he will give it to you. Until now you have not asked for anything in my name. Ask and you will receive, so that your joy may be complete.

"I have said these things to you in figures of speech. The hour is coming when I will no longer speak to you in figures, but will tell you plainly of the Father. On that day you will ask in my name. I do not say to you that I will ask the Father on your behalf; for the Father himself loves you, because you have loved me and have believed that I came from God. I came from the Father and have come into the world; again, I am leaving the world and am going to the Father."

His disciples said, "Yes, now you are speaking plainly, not in any figure of speech! Now we know that you know all things, and do not need to have anyone question you; by this we believe that you came from God." Jesus answered them, "Do you now believe? The hour is coming, indeed it has come, when you will be scattered, each one to his home, and you will leave me alone. Yet I am not alone because the Father is with me. I have said this to you, so that in me you may have peace. In the world you face persecution. But take courage; I have conquered the world!"

COMMENTARY

One of the more common Christian hopes is to have all of our questions answered by Christ when he returns for the second and final time. Yet in this passage, Jesus makes it clear that we won't have any questions when we see him again! Everything we were worried about, everyone we missed, will be resolved by his presence. In short, because Jesus has a future, so do we and all others who have loved him.

Again, the Father is lifted up and pointed to as Christ's goal and our lover. Though we may feel as lonely as Christ felt when abandoned by his disciples, neither he nor we are alone, because the Father is with us. The concluding claim of Jesus is nothing short of momentous; "I have conquered the world!" The exclamation point is his.

PRAYER 57

Lord Jesus Christ, you have heard us say to one another, over and over again, "When I get to heaven, the first thing I'm going to ask is ..." Now you tell us that won't be necessary. You tell us that all of those questions will dissipate instantly. You tell us that the mere sight of you will answer every question that ever haunted us.

If it happens as you promise, all will be "forgiven" us, for what are our questions, except doubt that you will keep your word? What difference will our questions of "Why?" or "How come?" make if you are there in resurrected glory to wake us from death and greet us with new life? With the beginning of eternity, with the gift of new bodies fit for a new life, what is there to ask? When all that we've lost has been renewed and restored forever, all the doubts will vanish more quickly than our dashed hopes in this world.

Lord Jesus, it hard to keep these thoughts in mind as we face the cruelty of losses so personal that no amount of imagination is sufficient to see us out of our dilemma. It is hard to live with one foot in this world, and one in the next. It is hard to believe that your kingdom has already come, yet is coming in still more glory. But if we don't believe these things, if like Paul we have hope only for this world, we are most to be pitied.

Lord Jesus, you say you have conquered the world! You say this before your crucifixion and before your resurrection. You say this as an accomplished historical fact, and all the words surrounding this bold claim are words about your loving Father. You tell us to ask him whatever we will, but he will respond, because of you. You tell us to ask him directly. You know that the cross is ahead for you, and that persecution must necessarily come to us if we follow you. You do not even tell us how to escape it. You simply dismiss it with, "Take courage, I have conquered the world!"

Lord Jesus, you have conquered the world because you have held on to the Father, and he has held on to you, with all the heart, mind, and soul there is on both sides of eternal life. Help us to do the same. Amen.

58. TOGETHER FOREVER

John 17:1-5
After Jesus had spoken these words, he looked up to heaven and said, "Father, the hour has come; glorify your Son so that the Son may glorify you, since you have given him authority over all people, to give eternal life to all whom you have given him. And this is eternal life, that they may know you, the one true God, and Jesus Christ whom you have sent. I glorified you on earth by finishing the work that you gave me to do. So now, Father, glorify me in your own presence with the glory that I had in your presence before the world existed."

COMMENTARY

"Glory" is a most difficult and dangerous concept. Commonly understood, it is praise and adoration. If we take it upon ourselves, it is not "glory" but "pride." If we believe we are worthy of it, then immediately unworthiness distills it like the morning dew. But when Jesus talks about glory, he is not talking about pomp or fame. He is talking about eternal life from the Father for us, and being in the presence of God the Father, again and forever.

PRAYER 58

Lord Jesus, we all hope for a little limelight once in a while, our moment upon the stage to be recognized for talent or worth. We have all kinds of ceremonies in place to give to one another recognition and glory. It starts early, Lord, this reward for good conduct and achievement. From the applause or hugs of our parents when we were toddlers, to this day, Lord, we yearn to be praiseworthy, acceptable, loved. If we don't get some praise, Lord, we don't have any self-esteem.

It's in all the books, Lord. We need to be valued. Someone has to see us and say, "You're nice," or "I like you." Without that affirmation, we are filled with self-doubt and loathing. It's purely psychological for most of us.

Lord Jesus, you talked about glory another way. It wasn't a psychological matter at all. You talked about eternal life as a gift from the Father for us through you. You said this in conversation with the Almighty. You talked about us with him. You based all your glory upon doing the Father's will, by coming to us as the gateway to eternal life.

And, Lord, you kept talking about being in the presence of the Father. You remembered what it was like before you came to be with us. You remembered being with the Father constantly, and in your prayer to the Father, you lifted up for us the vision of all of us being together forever — you, the Father, and us. You call this "glory," and so it is.

Lord, we can only understand glory in terms of this world, yet you knew what it was without this world, before this world. Your experience with glory precedes the day of creation. When there was only darkness and a void, from our perspective, you were there in glory with the Father. Marvel upon marvel, you now compare the glory of our being together with you in eternity to the glory you had with the Father before the creation of the world. You give us too much, Lord! We cannot grasp it. It is more glory than we can imagine. It is no mere moment upon the earth stage to strut our stuff; it is cosmic in scope, infinite in time, and relational in nature. We will be together forever.

Glorious, Lord, truly glorious. Thank you. Amen.

59. GOD-ESTEEM

John 17:6-19

"I have made your name known to those whom you gave me from the world. They were yours, and you gave them to me, and they have kept your word. Now they know that everything you have given me is from you; for the words that you gave to me I have given to them, and they have received them and know in truth that I came from you; and they have believed that you sent me. I am asking on their behalf; I am not asking on behalf of the world, but on behalf of those whom you gave me, because they are yours. All mine are yours, and yours are mine; and I have been glorified in them. And now I am no longer in the world, but they are in the world, and I am coming to you. Holy Father, protect them in your name that you have given me, so that they may be one, as we are one. While I was with them, I protected them in your name that you have given me. I guarded them, and not one of them was lost except the one destined to be lost, so that the scripture might be fulfilled. But now I am coming to you, and I speak these things in the world so that they may have my joy made complete in themselves. I have given them your word, and the world has hated them because they do not belong to the world, just as I do not belong to the world. I am not asking you to take them out of the world, but I ask you to protect them from the evil one. They do not belong to the world, just as I do not belong to the world. Sanctify them in the truth; your word is truth. As you have sent me into the world, so I have sent them into the world. And for their sakes I sanctify myself, so that they also may be sanctified in truth."

COMMENTARY

The words that we use in prayer reveal what is most important to us. These words of Jesus are his prayer words, and they are all about us and for us. The only way it is possible for us to know what Jesus said in this prayer was either for him to tell his disciples what he prayed, or for John to have overheard him in vocal prayer.

For reasons attributable only to love, we have become the apple of his eye. He reminds the Father how he has protected us from the evil one, has kept the disciples together as one, and he asks him to do the same for us. Jesus wants us to be unified in our mission to the world. He wants us to understand that we are sent people, just as he was sent to us. He speaks of us as though we are in the world, but not of it, and on that basis alone, joy is possible.

PRAYER 59

Lord Jesus Christ, you are the word-giver. You are the Word and you delivered the words given you by the Father. Because you have done this, you expect us to be in the world, but not of it, and to have a joy that is described as "full joy."

Lord, we Christians are often joyless in our demeanor and somber in our faith. We don't like the backslapping, ever-smiling Christians, who seemingly deny there is real pain and sorrow; nor do we like to be so gloomy ourselves that your spirit is always hidden behind a neutral face, if not a frown. We want to be authentic. We want to exhibit real love, not make-believe happiness. We don't want to be shallow in our knowledge or trite in our compassion.

What does peace look like on a Christian, Lord? Surely it is not glazed eyes and stoic smiles. Surely you don't want us to live lives of denial. Did you find peace on the night you prayed this prayer? You prayed these words on the same night you prayed in Gethsemane. There you had sweat on your forehead, like big drops of blood. You did not look serene.

Lord, we are all wrapped up in desire for self-esteem and peaceful thoughts. We want to think well of ourselves, even if others don't. We want to believe that we have proven ourselves to you as your lover, without bearing the cost of true discipleship; and if we have borne some of that cost, then we are apt to rely upon that suffering as our ticket to earned joy and peacefulness from you.

You won't let us get it that way, Lord. You keep pulling us away from our life experiences, tragic or blissful as they may have been to date, and you keep pointing at the cross and saying: "You need this. You need this death. Without it, you cannot be happy, cannot know joy, cannot be saved." You keep pointing at the cross and saying: "This is how much my Father would let me suffer, to convince you of your need of a Savior."

Lord, you won't let us save ourselves. Either you do it, or it isn't done. How humiliating. Our best efforts fall short. At the end, we have nothing to offer except a plea for mercy.

Lord Jesus, word-giver, listen to our prayers. Save us from ourselves. What good are we to you if we could save ourselves? How can we ever learn obedience if we can bypass the indignity of it all? How can you use us as your person, if we are still trying to do it all ourselves?

We know the answers to these questions. We just don't like the answers very much, because they feel demeaning. Yet you tell us that you listen, restore, and renew. You, the word-giver, have given your Word. On those promises, and by your cross, dear Savior, grant us peace. Amen.

60. TEAM EFFORT

John 17:20-26

"I ask not only on behalf of these, but also on behalf of those who will believe in me through their word, that they may all be one. As you, Father, are in me and I am in you, may they also be in us, so that the world may believe that you have sent me. The glory that you have given me I have given them, so that they may be one, as we are one, I in them and you in me, that they may become completely one, so that the world may know that you have sent me and have loved them even as you have loved me. Father, I desire that those also, whom you have given me, may be with me where I am, to see my glory, which you have given me because you loved me before the foundation of the world.

"Righteous Father, the world does not know you, but I know you; and these know that you have sent me. I made your name known to them, and I will make it known, so that the love with which you have loved me may be in them, and I in them."

COMMENTARY

Jesus continues to pray for us collectively. Despite all our attempts to individualize the faith to the point of privatizing our relationship to God, Jesus' prayer is for *us* to be one *together.*

PRAYER 60

Lord Jesus Christ, you have a big problem on your hands in this church of the millennium. We come before you, one by one, seeking out very personal relationships with you, without regard for the ways you have promised to come to us collectively. We prefer private prayer to public prayer. We want a private audience with you, on a regular basis, and prefer this time with you in prayer alone over your sacramental promises, where you come to us as we gather together. So much of our quest for you is a selfish quest, for our own comforting and hope, and not for the sake of our neighbors or your world.

Lord, you prayed for us to be one, together, not that we should be loners in the faith. Help us balance these important times alone with you, with quality time together with other sojourners, that our faith may be increased through the witness of others, and that the world may see you beyond the meditations of our own minds.

Lord, your church is in trouble. We are wandering aimlessly. We are not one. We care much more about our own personal faith journeys than we do about the unchurched. It has become unpopular to talk about bringing the nonbelievers to faith. We no longer worry much about them. We hardly know how to rejoice over adult baptisms because they are so rare. We argue over definitions and theologies, over process and motives, over personalities and goals, and seldom do the work of an evangelist. We claim we don't know how, and that is true. We have lost the courage to name your name to a friend, so private have we made our ever-so-slowly developing faiths. We have not hidden your house of worship, but we are compelling no one to come in.

How can we do it better, Lord? We know there is much nonbelief among us in the pew. We know there is plenty of work to do among our own memberships. We know that most of us prefer to rework the troops than to find new recruits. We know that the goal ought not to be church membership, but love of you and the Father. We are able to discuss these matters with passion, and to exhaustion, but we seem to be stuck in our easy chairs, unable to know how to make your presence among us "compelling."

Can it be, Lord, that we are not yet converted ourselves? Can it be that we still have such immature faiths that we have no ability to talk about you in confidence to another?

Lord, you always sent out your disciples in twos so that one could encourage another, and the faith could be something more than a single person's witness. We are afraid that our witness of your presence in our lives will sound weak and unimportant. A stranger's rejection of us devastates us, so we take no risk for you. Our faiths are so personal and fragile, we think it is us they are rejecting, not you. Lord, we need one another for more than companionship. We need a team effort, a church effort. We need one another for the sake of courage.

Lord, you told the Father that the world does not know him, but that you do. You tell us that if we know you, we also know the

Father. Grant us courage to believe this, and more courage to act upon it. May others join with us in the fellowship of believers. May our song of praise be no solo. May we sing together, with all the company of heaven. Amen.

61. FOR THE FATHER AND US

John 18:1-14

After Jesus had spoken these words, he went out with his disciples across the Kidron valley to a place where there was a garden, which he and his disciples entered. Now Judas, who betrayed him, also knew the place, because Jesus often met there with his disciples. So Judas brought a detachment of soldiers together with police from the chief priests and the Pharisees, and they came there with lanterns and torches and weapons. Then Jesus, knowing all that was to happen to him, came forward and asked them, "Whom are you looking for?" They answered, "Jesus of Nazareth." Jesus replied, "I am he." Judas, who betrayed him, was standing with them. When Jesus said to them, "I am he," they stepped back and fell to the ground. Again he asked them, "Whom are you looking for?" And they said, "Jesus of Nazareth." Jesus answered, "I told you that I am he. So if you are looking for me, let these men go." This was to fulfill the word that he had spoken, "I did not lose a single one of those whom you gave me." Then Simon Peter, who had a sword, drew it, struck the high priest's slave, and cut off his right ear. The slave's name was Malchus. Jesus said to Peter, "Put your sword back into its sheath. Am I not to drink the cup that the Father has given me?"

So the soldiers, their officer, and the Jewish police arrested Jesus and bound him. First they took him to Annas, who was the father-in-law of Caiaphas, the high priest that year. Caiaphas was the one who had advised the Jews that it was better to have one person die for the people.

COMMENTARY

That weapons, soldiers, and police were brought together to arrest Jesus, the Prince of Peace, is a fitting contrast between the kingdom of this world and the Kingdom of God.

That the arresters "fell back," unable to arrest Jesus without his permission, is the first indication that Jesus would do the Father's will, regardless of the cost. This is also verbalized to Peter. Finally, Peter's audacious attack upon Malchus, the priest's slave, is testimony both to Peter's willingness to die in battle for Christ, and his misunderstanding of Jesus' mission.

PRAYER 61

Lord Jesus, they bound you up, after you let them, like a common outlaw. It was probably standard arresting procedure even then. They tied you up, with a tether, without any notion of how ludicrous it is to try to tie up the Son of God, but you let them think they had you bound. You traded your freedom for the disciples' freedom. Your first church could have been all but eliminated that night, had you not gone peaceably.

Lord Jesus, you weren't willingly arrested just for the disciples' skin. You did this for the Father and for us. You knew what had to be, if ever we were to see Love's love. There was nothing in it for you, except love. Nothing at all. Nothing.

Lord, teach us to love like you. We know the doctrine, so it's not more understanding that we need, as though we'd *do* love if we only understood it better. We've played that game with you for years. Instead, teach us beyond the musings of our minds, and touch our hearts. Open up our souls to love. Open up our wills to love, so that we might be truly transformed. Open up our eyes to see you really here, among us, doing godly things.

This world, Lord, has no desire for you. This world, Lord, is satisfied with what it is. It has no vision, no sense of mystery. We do not seek the flame that transforms the will into something new. We do not want to be changed. We are tired of metaphor and illusion and things of the spirit. It is all too hard a work for us to do. We want light only as illumination of things, not as the Way to walk. We are so satisfied with loneliness that we deny our relationship to you, to light, to others, to earth itself.

Lord Jesus, you put us here for the sake of experience, and we are afraid to have it. You put us into physical form so that we might see both beauty and tragedy from the inside, and not as some mere gazing tourist. You have worlds in countless galaxies throughout the universe, but what does it matter if no one can see the magnitude of their beauty and their problems from the inside? You want us to know life in its physical form, as well as in its spiritual form, but we are running from both experiences, because we are afraid of pain and suffering and learning. We are afraid of you, Lord Jesus, because you want so much, love so ardently, give so readily, die so willingly.

You went to the cross to show us the way, not just to teach us about your way. You went to the cross for the sake of obedience. You went because it was your Father's will, not your own. You went so that we may find a way to live beyond the shallowness of the world. You went to the cross to let us know that there is more to come, even after this day's work is done. You went to make us partners with you throughout eternity, for the sake of the cosmos. You went, and you promise us that we will follow. Amen.

62. LITTLE MATTERS THAT MATTERED

John 18:15-27

Simon Peter and another disciple followed Jesus. Since that disciple was known to the high priest, he went with Jesus into the courtyard of the high priest, but Peter was standing outside at the gate. So the other disciple, who was known to the high priest, went out, spoke to the woman who guarded the gate, and brought Peter in. The woman said to Peter, "You are not also one of this man's disciples, are you?" He said, "I am not." Now the slaves and the police had made a charcoal fire, because it was cold, and they were standing around it and warming themselves. Peter also was standing with them and warming himself.

Then the high priest questioned Jesus about his disciples and about his teaching. Jesus answered, "I have spoken openly to the world; I have always taught in synagogues and in the temple, where all the Jews come together. I have said nothing in secret. Why do you ask me? Ask those who heard what I said to them; they know what I said." When he had said this, one of the police standing nearby struck Jesus on the face, saying, "Is that how you answer the high priest?" Jesus answered, "If I have spoken wrongly, testify to the wrong. But if I have spoken rightly, why do you strike me?" Then Annas sent him bound to Caiaphas the high priest.

Now Simon Peter was standing and warming himself. They asked him, "You are not also one of his disciples, are you?" He denied it and said, "I am not." One of the slaves of the high priest, a relative of the man whose ear Peter had cut off, asked, "Did I not see you in the garden with him?" Again Peter denied it, and at that moment the cock crowed.

COMMENTARY

Still bound, Jesus is questioned about his teaching *and* his disciples. His disciples were in danger, so Jesus speaks only about his teaching. It is a significant matter, for Jesus is protecting them even now.

Often the church has ridiculed the fearful disciples, but they had reason to be afraid. Judas, in effect, betrayed not only the Lord, but his colleagues as well. They were all marked men, but Jesus counseled for their release by his surrender and partial answering of the high priest's questions.

PRAYER 62

Lord Jesus, when you were asked about the disciples, what thoughts went through your head? You knew that they were in danger. You knew where they would be hiding. You simply ignored the high priest's question and went on to the one about your teachings. You did this for them, Lord. You protected your disciples, and because you did, you saved your loyal lovers until you could be back with them after death. You saved the first church from premature extinction.

Lord, you were slapped across the face by a soldier who didn't like your answers. He didn't like you, Lord. He thought you were trouble. We know what that is like. We know what's it like to be mistreated, slandered, talked about, and deliberately "misunderstood." You weren't silent with the slap, Lord. You defended yourself a little. You gave guidance to your assailants, but they didn't listen. Assailants seldom do.

Lord Jesus Christ, you let that slapper go. You could have humiliated him with words, struck him down with a curse, or ignored him entirely, but you didn't. You answered him. You acknowledged his existence, and you questioned his deed. All of his life he would have to wonder about the day he slapped the man who was sent from God to defeat death. All of his life, he would have to live with his impulse. But maybe, Lord, he never gave it another thought. Maybe, like us, when we wound another needlessly, we forget our impulsiveness.

Peter was denying you, Lord, while all of this was going on. It was not a good time for him to make a witness about you. He wanted to be near you. He didn't want to be arrested yet. What good would he be to you if he were also bound? He might yet spring you out, when a guard wasn't looking. It was a "little" denial. It was sensible. He needed to be around for a bigger moment, a better day, a greater crowd of would-be believers. Why waste himself with the careless truth to a woman guard? She didn't want to know if he was a believer for faith's sake, but only to give him trouble.

Yes, Lord, it was still a denial, but an understandable one. We get ourselves into difficulties like this all the time. There are places and moments where a witness about you isn't very helpful to anyone. You understand that, don't you? Yes, Lord, we know. It happened again. Then again. And the cock crowed loudly. Poor Peter.

Lord, forgive us all as we look for the perfect moment to be your person, instead of the moment that comes when it comes. Forgive us our desire to try to be opportunists, to figure out the best time to show our faith, to think that little moments don't matter. Infiltrate our lives so thoroughly with your way that thoughts about when to witness about you aren't even asked. Lord Jesus, you never denied who you were. Why should we? Grant us your courage, O Lord, to take the slap and keep on talking. Amen.

63. MEMBERSHIP IN ANOTHER WORLD

John 18:28-40
Then they took Jesus from Caiaphas to Pilate's headquarters. It was early in the morning. They themselves did not enter the headquarters, so as to avoid ritual defilement and to be able to eat the Passover. So Pilate went out to them and said, "What accusations do you bring against this man?" They answered, "If this man were not a criminal, we would not have handed him over to you." Pilate said to them, "Take him yourselves and judge him according to your law." The Jews replied, "We are not permitted to put anyone to death." (This was to fulfill what Jesus had said when he indicated the kind of death he was to die.)

Then Pilate entered the headquarters again, summoned Jesus, and asked him, "Are you the King of the Jews?" Jesus answered, "Do you ask this on your own, or did others tell you about me?" Pilate replied, "I am not a Jew, am I? Your own nation and the chief priests have handed you over to me. What have you done?" Jesus answered, "My kingdom is not from this world. If my kingdom were from this world, my followers would be fighting to keep me from being handed over to the Jews. But as it is, my kingdom is not from here." Pilate asked him, "So you are a king?" Jesus answered, "You say that I am a king. For this I was born, and for this I came into the world, to testify to the truth. Everyone who belongs to the truth listens to my voice." Pilate asked him, "What is truth?"

After he had said this, he went out to the Jews again and told them, "I find no case against him. But you have a custom that I release someone for you at the Passover. Do you want me to release for you the King of the Jews?" They shouted in reply, "Not this man, but Barabbas!" Now Barabbas was a bandit.

COMMENTARY

Pilate was the key to a death sentence, as Jesus was passed from Annas to Caiaphas to Pilate. Everything was being done in "good order," but Pilate was the only one with authority to have a man crucified.

All the talk about a kingship intrigued Pilate. He knew no king could live within the Roman empire, except the emperor, and when Jesus admitted to having a kingship of truth from another world, made up of those who listen to his voice, Pilate had to ask, "What is truth?"

Pilate, willing to satiate their lust for blood, thought he had a political solution to the problem. He would offer up Barabbas in place of the "king," and he would be rid of a troublemaker, while Jesus could continue to rule in a kingship from another world; but it all backfired.

PRAYER 63

Lord Jesus Christ, you should have had legal counsel. Everyone knew that one didn't admit to being a king on Roman territory. All you had to do was explain yourself a little. You should have told Pilate how you had come from another world to teach the residents of this world how to live good lives. You should have told Pilate that you meant no harm, were purely religious, and would not interfere with earthly things. You should not play with words with Pilate. He had the power to say the word to let you go.

We know, Lord, that this is only the appearance of things from the rational point of view. We know that nothing could have stopped your crucifixion — not a good governor, not a bad Barabbas, not even the truth. They were going to have you dead by nightfall, and neither the Heavenly Father nor you were going to stop it.

Pilate asked you, the Truth, "What is truth?" Looking right into your eyes he could not see it. He had no memory of your saying, "I am the truth." He didn't know what to look for. Truth for him, like for most of us, was just some vague concept; but he knew it was a tricky concept. He knew that it was slippery and that he had seen little, if any, of it in his lifetime. He knew enough to be a cynic and skeptic about it.

Lord Jesus, if you are the Truth, then you change all our thinking about truth as being some sort of explanation, some sort of statement of fact. You replace all that head work with yourself as reality, as gospel, as the ultimate fact of life, beyond example, beyond explanation, and beyond understanding. You, as person, as heart, as God in flesh, are truth incarnate as well as love incarnate. You are the only way to make any sense at all out of this mad and crazy truth-evading world. You, Lord, either were, are, and will be, or nothing makes sense. Nothing. Nothing at all. If you are false, life is false, and there is no truth to be had, no morality to attain, no life to come, no God at all. Lord Jesus, if you are not king, queen, emperor, and ruler, there is no order, no purpose, no justice, and no family on earth worth membership. Without you, Lord, this world is all lost forever, an illusion with no more power than a desert mirage.

Lord, help us to understand that our membership in your kingdom is membership in another world. Help us to understand that your kingdom has come and is coming; that it has come as invader with your birth, and will come in full power on the last day. Help us look forward in joy to the day of fullness, so that these days of suffering are put into proper perspective. Help us see that all that afflicts us now is passing away and will be gone forever when you come as king forever. Amen.

64. LOOKING AT US WITH LOVE

John 19:1-7
Then Pilate took Jesus and had him flogged. And the soldiers wove a crown of thorns and put it on his head, and they dressed him in a purple robe. They kept coming up to him, saying, "Hail, King of the Jews!" and striking him on the face. Pilate went out again and said to them, "Look, I am bringing him out to you to let you know that I find no case against him." So Jesus came out, wearing the crown of thorns and the purple robe. Pilate said to them, "Here is the man!" When the chief priests and the police saw him, they shouted, "Crucify him! Crucify him!" Pilate said to them, "Take him yourselves and crucify him; I find no case against him." The Jews answered him, "We have a law, and according to that law he ought to die because he has claimed to be the Son of God."

COMMENTARY

The judgment of Pilate was right: "I find no case against him." Now Jesus becomes every man, woman, or child who is punished innocently, abused, or who suffers injustice. Now we know we have a God who knows what it's like to be "done wrong."

That the world is cruel is evidenced in this passage. Only a fool or a love beyond understanding would go on to the cross after this mocking. It is, of course, "the love that passes all understanding" that will not let us go, regardless of the cost.

PRAYER 64

"What language shall we borrow" to see the sorrow of this day? You were held in contempt, Lord Jesus Christ; you were loathed. The crown of thorns and purple robe made sure you knew what they thought of you. It wasn't your teaching, Lord, they hated. It was you. It was your Father, too, whom they taunted with those slaps across your face, a Father they didn't know. They had no fear of either of you, for they had no faith in either of you.

What did you represent to the multitude? Change? Perhaps, but maybe something more, something greater. Lord Jesus, you had to be shown that you are no better than the rest of us. Lord

Jesus, we don't like other people thinking more of themselves than they ought to think.

Lord Jesus, you didn't discourage the talk about kingship. Worse than that, you made yourself one with the Father. You said that you and he were partners in your ministry, and that you did what he told you to do. You dished out bread and called it your body. You served wine and called it your blood. You said that we could be friends with God, not merely servants. The list is endless.

You did too many miracles. You healed, but there were always the cynics doubting that it was so. You raised stinking people from the dead, because death flees from your presence, but that was too much for the orthodox of any age to believe. For your sake, you would have been better off without the signs.

So here we are, Lord, in prayer with you. Here we are as orthodox, cynic, doubter, and sometimes friend. We see the slap and wonder how you'll react. The thorns and robe mock you well. If this happens to you, Lord, what will happen to us if we follow? What did you expect your crucifixion to do, Lord, make people line up to die a gruesome death? We get the lesson you were being taught. We understand the message. Follow you and there will be a price to pay. Big price.

But, Lord, what other alternative do we have? Even without the resurrection, you are irresistible. You have a way of getting inside of us, like a deep ache in the throat, that lets us know we have been touched by something holy. You captivate us, Lord. You grab us with your Spirit, your Holy Spirit, and our spirits can't resist you. We find courage where before there was only fear, joy where sadness reigned, hope where despair had won the day. How can this be, robed and crowned like a fool? How can you affect us looking like this?

Lord Jesus, don't answer the question, just look at us one at a time. Let us see you looking at us in love. Make us see you. Move us away from our obvious shortcomings, and make us see you looking at us with love.

Fill us with resolve to be about the Father's business, with little thought of the cost. Big price? So what. Bigger heart! That's what we see when we see you. That's what won't let us go — you looking at us with love. Amen.

65. NO DECISION AT ALL

John 19:8-16a

Now when Pilate heard this, he was more afraid than ever. He entered his headquarters again and asked Jesus, "Where are you from?" But Jesus gave him no answer. Pilate therefore said to him, "Do you refuse to speak to me? Do you not know that I have power to release you, and power to crucify you?" Jesus answered him, "You would have no power over me unless it had been given you from above; therefore the one who handed me over to you is guilty of a greater sin." From then on Pilate tried to release him, but the Jews cried out, "If you release this man, you are no friend of the emperor. Everyone who claims to be a king sets himself against the emperor."

When Pilate heard these words, he brought Jesus outside and sat on the judge's bench at a place called The Stone Pavement, or in Hebrew Gabbatha. Now it was the day of Preparation for the Passover; and it was about noon. He said to the Jews, "Here is your King!" They cried out, "Away with him! Away with him! Crucify him!" Pilate asked them, "Shall I crucify your King?" The chief priests answered, "We have no king but the emperor." Then he handed him over to them to be crucified.

COMMENTARY

Perhaps there is no other event in the world that shows the limitation of majority rule as this event. Minds were made up, and no amount of persuasion or reason would undo it. Pilate genuinely tried to have Jesus freed, but the passion of tradition and culture often blinds us to the presence of God among us in any capacity.

The cleverness of adversaries can overwhelm the truth, even truth incarnate, for a day. The horridness and stupidity of sin is not that it is unsuccessful, but precisely because it succeeds. The day belonged to sin, but the day of the Lord was coming.

PRAYER 65

Lord Jesus, Pontius Pilate was in such a predicament. He knew you were innocent. He knew the power of enraged people and the importance of appeasement. He wasn't willing to give up the governorship for you at your first meeting. He had no idea that this event would put him in the history books and the creeds forever. Of all the good things in life he may have done, this is what he's remembered for. He's remembered for being savvy, for struggling with the issue, but collapsing under pressure. He's remembered for going against his own conscience, for the sake of the people.

He didn't understand power, Lord, except it meant "being in charge." He knew he had responsibility to make a decision, but he was hustled into one prematurely. It all came down to prudence. His good common sense was blocked at every avenue of exit by committed religionists. They sounded sincere. They said the right things. They knew what strings to pull on him. They knew that Pilate knew that Rome would investigate if he faltered. How sinister is faith based on power. They prevailed and got their way. They got you, Lord Jesus, because Pilate was trained to be prudent, not wise.

Every day, Lord, we are faced with conditions and situations too complex for us to understand. The mob shouts one thing at us, but our conscience whispers something else. We are afraid to trust our own instincts, even when they've been formed by your teachings and presence. We are not yet free from the judgment of the world that claims to be as wise as you. Besides, we like the world. The world is quick to forgive things we like to do — quick to forgive war, quick to ignore adultery, quick to forgive selfishness. The world understands our need for these things.

Lord Jesus, if we were ever to follow you completely, we wouldn't recognize ourselves. We wouldn't be who we are today. You would make us make other decisions, and you would let us bear the consequences for them. You got yourself killed doing things this way.

We struggle mightily with you, Lord Jesus, because we don't want to volunteer for martyrdom. We have limited strength to follow you all on our own. We do need to be savvy, too. We have to be credible in this world. You do want us to love one another, don't you, and support one another?

In all of these rationalizations, Lord, you pull back the screen of self-delusion. You know that we can't follow you one step without your constant call and urging. You know we would have already turned back, if it were only our own strength available for the journey. You know that the Father was with you before Pilate, and that all the world's history was being changed through your conversation with him. You know all that we really need for this time and place, including credibility. You are not worried about our true love for one another, just false love that capitulates to mob thinking, worldly wisdom.

Lord Jesus, we need you with us every step of the way, just as you needed the strength of a lifetime experience with the Father. We need to build up our faith in you now, so that the day of decision to be your person will be automatic, so that it will be no decision at all, but you in us, doing the Father's will. We need to know you, Lord Jesus, not only as teacher, but as constant companion. To that end, walk with us today, and show us the Father. Amen.

66. KING JESUS

John 19:16b-25a

So they took Jesus; and carrying the cross by himself, he went out to what is called The Place of the Skull, which in Hebrew is called Golgotha. There they crucified him, and with him two others, one on either side, with Jesus between them. Pilate also had an inscription written and put on the cross. It read, "Jesus of Nazareth, the King of the Jews." Many of the Jews read this inscription, because the place where Jesus was crucified was near the city; and it was written in Hebrew, in Latin, and in Greek. Then the chief priests of the Jews said to Pilate, "Do not write, 'The King of the Jews,' but, 'This man said, I am King of the Jews.'" Pilate answered, "What I have written I have written." When the soldiers had crucified Jesus, they took his clothes and divided them into four parts, one for each soldier. They also took his tunic; now the tunic was seamless, woven in one piece from the top. So they said to one another, "Let us not tear it, but cast lots for it to see who will get it." This was to fulfill what the scripture says, "They divided my clothes among themselves, and for my clothing they cast lots." And that is what the soldiers did.

COMMENTARY

This passage tells what Pilate did and what the soldiers did when Jesus was crucified. Pilate finally said no to the religious leaders, and he would not change his mind regarding what he had written. To this day, the truth of what he wrote, "The King of the Jews," stands as testimony. It shall not go away, because Jesus won't go away.

The soldiers, meanwhile, are entrepreneurs. They recognized the value of the robe but could not see the Christ, from whom it came. Earlier, Pilate looked at truth in the eye and asked "What is truth?" It is a part of our sickness to see the value of a thing, or ask the right question, but still miss the ultimate reality.

PRAYER 66

Although he didn't free you as he should have, Lord, Pilate did the next best thing. With resolute determination he announced to the whole world that you are King. He said it in multiple languages. He said it short and to the point. Having been backed into the corner of a bad decision, he came out swinging. He announced it to all the world. He proclaimed you King. He said more than he probably knew, but he said it, whether in anger toward the leaders who brought you before him, or in defense of his decision. It doesn't matter. You are King.

King Jesus. The title isn't royal enough. You carried the cross alone, when disciples and followers should have swarmed to your aid. Though your companions on the cross were thieves, you made no complaint about the humiliation you were suffering. Your tunic became the prize for a roll of the dice, because, they thought, you would never use clothes again. But, King Jesus, your reign was just beginning. From here on out the miracle seekers who liked to be amazed, and the romantics, who like nice truths told in pleasant parables, will have to add this horrendous moment to their inclination to follow you. From now on, naivete won't get it. You are about blood and shame, dying and giving, suffering and doing. You won't be had as sentimentality. You are for real. You are the one and only King. Amen.

67. LET DEATH COME, LORD JESUS

John 19:25b-27

Meanwhile, standing near the cross of Jesus were his mother, and his mother's sister, Mary the wife of Clopas, and Mary Magdalene. When Jesus saw his mother and the disciple whom he loved standing beside her, he said to his mother, "Woman, here is your son." Then he said to the disciple, "Here is your mother." and from that hour the disciple took her into his own home.

COMMENTARY

It was three Marys, and probably John, the author of the Gospel we are praying through, who made up this holy foursome with Jesus. John was the one disciple who had enough courage to be there. He probably went there in great fear for his personal safety. Certainly, he had no thought for what he was about to be given — care for the mother of our Lord. Obviously, he didn't know that this would happen before he went before the cross.

Jesus gives, even while dying, to those who come before his cross. From that cruel moment, grace flowed, not only for Mary, but also for John. He was selected to live with the most divinely blessed of all human beings, she who was called to birth Jesus. It was right that they should both be there beneath the cross.

PRAYER 67

Lord Jesus, did you see your mother's pain for you from the cross? Did you feel her utter sense of hopelessness? Do you know what it's like to be a parent with a dying child, dying before your very eyes, with no power but prayer? Do you know what it's like to lose one's nearest and dearest?

We know that you were not sent to earth to be a parent, Lord Jesus, but sent to be among us who have seen so many devastations: children with disease who were born from love, the trauma of an accident, the violent shedding of another's blood, the suicide of one's beloved. The testimony is sure: nothing is more painful than the loss of one whom we love, not even our own impending deaths.

Lord, do you see Mary watching you die? That is us looking at our sick or dying loved ones, not with mere pity and hopelessness, but with confusion and anger and pain so sharp that we can't even think clearly. Nothing makes sense, if death is this powerful. No plan for a future has purpose if death can annihilate love like this in an instant. No amount of courage can overcome the dread of death for our beloved ones.

Do you see Mary your mother looking at you, Lord? It may be your cross, your nails, and your crown, but you were her son, and that cross is killing her too, splitting her heart like a sharp two-edged sword. It doesn't matter that this was predicted ahead of time. The hour for her soul to be pierced because of your death is worse than the hour of her own dying. We do not pretend to bravery and sacrifice when we say, "Take me and spare my loved one." We know that you make no deals like this, but the offer is our way of saying that this is unbearable pain, worse than personal death.

Lord, you must have seen her suffering. You must have felt incredible pathos for your inability not to die, not to do the Father's will, even for her sake. Surely, for her, you would want to step back from death and live, but you were just as powerless as she. You were facing each other with pure helplessness between you. Nothing good could come from this, yet you said, "Mary, John is your son. John, Mary is your mother." You placed both of them into a new relationship with one another. You gave to both someone dear to you. You gave someone with flesh and blood to share the memory of this awful moment, and the joys of better days yet to come, though no mortal eye could yet see them.

Lord Jesus, this terrible moment on the cross gave you the experience we want you to have about our intense love for one another, and what it takes to let a loved one go. We are not glad that you had to suffer like this, for you did not deserve it, but we are glad that you know what it's like to wish with all your heart, like us, that the horrible pain before our eyes would go away, that a miracle would occur, that our beloved could know our heart and feel our love, and by that power, undo the moment.

We need a Savior, Lord Jesus. Nothing less will do. Our love, though complete, is not enough. Our courage, though reckless with daring, is not enough. Our experience, though filled with ardor and compassion, is not enough. Something greater needs to face death for us and make it run in fear of itself. Only you can do this, Lord Jesus. Do not come down from the cross. Not yet. Let death come. Let it take you to the realm of the dead, and then, Lord Jesus, show it your power. Do it for Mary. Do it for John. Do it for those we love. Do it for us. Amen.

68. ACCOMPLISHED

John 19:28-30
After this, when Jesus knew that all was now finished, he said (in order to fulfill the Scripture), "I am thirsty." A jar full of sour wine was standing there. So they put a sponge full of the wine on a branch of hyssop and held it to his mouth. When Jesus had received the wine, he said, "It is finished." Then he bowed his head and gave up his spirit.

COMMENTARY

He who entered the river with John the Baptist, and called himself "living water," was thirsty. He who passed the chalice on the previous night telling all to drink, is now thirsty. Perhaps he did it just to fulfill the Scriptures, but doubtlessly his humanness was also saying that he was dehydrated unto death.

"It is finished" was a cry of triumph, not a weak pathetic cry of resignation that his life was now over. It was the victory cry of having been faithful to the Father's will to the end, of going into the realm of the dead to do death in, and his coming home at last.

PRAYER 68

If there is ever any doubt about it, Lord, your thirst on the cross for something to drink is validation that you are one of us. You cry like us, eat like us, pray like us, thirst like us, and die like us. You know what we are going through with every bodily experience. You have felt the heat of the day and the physical pain of suffering. You know what others can do to our bodies, whether on a day of crucifixion, or in a lifetime of stress and lovelessness. You know the limitations of the flesh and the need for a new body, fit for a new life in a new world.

You were thirsty, Lord, and we like to imagine that we would hold the cup to your lips had we been there at that moment, but that is mostly a romantic notion. Your parched lips are still found everywhere on the earth where famine strikes and people thirst. We with the food don't notice enough. We hardly notice the hungry as our sister or brother.

You are thirsty, Lord, even today. You are thirsty for justice, for food, for shelter, for health care, for the basics of a healthy life for all your creatures, but we keep looking at the price tag. And, if all of us get those precious things, we still have more than a little tendency not to thank you for them. They become our right, our privilege, our due. You keep making your newest followers from among the poor who live without what they need, rather than from us who think we don't need you anymore, except for catastrophic illness. Few of us pray for rain or harvest and mean it. Few of us know what it's like to ask you to stretch out your hands over a parched continent and gather the clouds together so that food may grow. We don't even pray for health until we've been to the doctor for advice. The better you are to us, Lord, the farther from you we roam. We are your spoiled ones.

Lord Jesus, you were thirsty and, despite that cosmic thirst of yours, you said triumphantly, "It is finished." Your experience as one of us was done. Your completion of your mission was over. You were going to the realm of the dead to show your power and free the captives. You were on your way to the home from which you came. Finished! Done! Accomplished! No one cheered you then, Lord Jesus, because no one understood the magnitude of the sacrifice they had witnessed. No one understood that the Lamb was slain. No one saw that the veins that opened in your hands and feet are still pouring blood into countless chalices forever, the sacramental offering of yourself for us. No one knew, Lord, so no one sang.

Your head sagged forward and fell upon your chest. You looked defeated, Lord Jesus. Perhaps you were setting the trap for death and Satan, to surprise them both in the realm of the dead, but for now you were as dead as dead gets. Your victory wasn't indicated by hands raised in triumph, fists striking at empty air, and shouts of joy, but rather a head bent, yielding, yielding, yielding to the needs of others. You did this out of love for us. You didn't need to whip up our emotions with daring feats of bravado. You did it all by yielding. You did it all, thirsty and yielding. To this day the world sees only defeat.

Lord Jesus, we cannot ever match your love, but we can yield for the sake of another. In so doing, you promise a benefit for ourselves, even if it's only in knowing that it pleases you. Be for us, Lord Jesus, what the Father was for you, our reason for living differently from the world, while still in the world. Amen.

69. BLOOD AND WATER

John 19:31-37

Since it was the day of Preparation, the Jews did not want the bodies left on the cross during the sabbath, especially because that sabbath was a day of great solemnity. So they asked Pilate to have the legs of the crucified men broken and the bodies removed. Then the soldiers came and broke the legs of the first and of the other who had been crucified with him. But when they came to Jesus and saw that he was already dead, they did not break his legs. Instead, one of the soldiers pierced his side with a spear, and at once blood and water came out. (He who saw this has testified so that you also may believe. His testimony is true, and he knows that he tells the truth.) These things occurred so that the scripture might be fulfilled, "None of his bones shall be broken." And again another passage of scripture says, "They will look on the one whom they have pierced."

COMMENTARY

The piercing of Jesus' body with a spear was also the piercing of Mary's soul. Her beloved son must now become the beloved Son of God. He has become her Savior, even as he has become the Savior of the world.

The blood and water that poured from the side of Jesus are also the primary elements used in the sacraments — the water of baptism and the blood of the Holy Eucharist. Both are literally poured out for us from Christ.

PRAYER 69

Lord Jesus Christ, on top of that hill, in plain view of every person with morbid curiosity, hate, or love, one spear was thrust openly into your side. There was no privacy for you. Like a lamb in the field, you were slaughtered. One deep jab and blood and water flowed out upon this earth, staining this globe, and hallowing it forever. You died here. You let the life forces of yourself as the Son of God pour out here. The central object of your creation, this place called "good" when the work was done, became the place of your dying.

The gruesomeness of your death, Lord Jesus, is not the physical cruelty of it all. We are used to seeing mangled bodies and corpses from war and accident, although it is always repulsive. The gruesomeness, Lord, is that this was you, that you were the one obedient human being, that you had no business dying, because you never absented yourself from the presence of the Father. You did everything you were told by him. You listened to every word that came and even drank the cruel death of crucifixion. Now you are being killed like a thief, executed like a sinner, and all because of us.

It is hard to understand, Lord, why all of this was necessary. Why did the Father exact such a death from his own beloved? Is it only because if he spared you, we would not ever really believe? Is it Lucifer plying his wares on you one last time? Is it to get into the realm of the dead, and from there free the bodies and souls of those who looked forward to your coming in faith?

It is all too mysterious for us to comprehend, Lord Jesus. You let all of this happen, and now we cannot even begin to fathom the depth of principalities and powers that were eternally affected by your dying. We know little of the angels and archangels that trembled at this moment. We've heard of cherubim and seraphim, but we don't know what they were doing when the blood and water spilled out. We can only imagine the cry of anguish from your Father reverberating throughout the cosmos. What you did here affects everything everywhere, from here to the most distant star, from here to the most distant heart. You have managed to penetrate every living thing, like a spear into the side of yourself.

Lord, may we see this pouring out of yourself every time we see the chalice filled at the Holy Communion. May we see your vein opened up to feed us. May we taste the wine of Communion and understand that this blood is from the Son of God's resurrected body. May we taste the bread and know it is your flesh from another realm, entering yet the physical bodies of us, your people, whom you have come to save. May we know that you are still both part of our souls and part of our bodies, cell of our cells as well as spirit of our spirits.

All of this dying, Lord, is telling us that when our hour comes, you will know what is happening. You have felt the fear, the pain, the uncertainty. All of your dying, Lord, is saying personally to us, "Do not be afraid, I have already done this, and I am not going to let you die alone." All of your agony, Lord, lessens ours, because you are faithful to your promise to help us pass through the moment into the bright light of eternal life.

Lord Jesus Christ, thank you for dying. Thank you for dying for us. Thank you for experiencing every raw moment, so that our individual moments of death may only be passages from the world of faith to the world of eternal partnership with you. Amen.

70. CEMETERY

John 19:38-42
After these things, Joseph of Arimathea, who was a disciple of Jesus, though a secret one because of his fear of the Jews, asked Pilate to let him take away the body of Jesus. Pilate gave him permission; so he came and removed the body. Nicodemus, who had at first come to Jesus by night, also came, bringing a mixture of myrrh and aloes, weighing about a hundred pounds. They took the body of Jesus and wrapped it with the spices in linen cloths, according to the burial custom of the Jews. Now there was a garden in the place where he was crucified, and in the garden there was a new tomb in which no one had ever been laid. And so, because it was the Jewish day of Preparation, and the tomb was nearby, they laid Jesus there.

COMMENTARY

After all of the teaching, healing, and living among the faithful disciples, the disposition of the body of Jesus is cared for by a rich believer, Joseph of Arimathea, who was afraid of publicly showing his faith, and Nicodemus, the one who came secretly to Jesus at night, asking questions about the kingdom of God. In a sense, the faith is always an underground movement. It infiltrates the world, despite all the pressures of the world to annihilate it.

Now that Jesus has been laid to rest, like every mortal, even the tombs in which we lie are sanctified. There is no place from which God cannot work, including our graves.

PRAYER 70

Now we are there, Lord Jesus, at that dread place called "cemetery." It's not that we love our bodies so much that we cannot bear the thought of their burials or their returning to the earth from which they came. It's more the awful thought of the darkness in a box, the awful thought of decay, of being powerless ever to breathe again, walk again, or use any sense we've been granted use of while here. Now we are at your tomb, with a hundred pounds of spices to cover up the quick deterioration of flesh without life. Now we are there with a heavy heart, seeing that your life has ended like all others.

Lord, we think of those special spots on earth, the graves of our loved ones, and we wonder about our own spot yet to come. Who will be there to say farewell and shed a tear of grief? Who will have to do this dirty work of disposing of our corrupt flesh, unable to live anymore? What will the first day of life on earth be like after we are gone? If it weren't for the history books, we would scarcely believe that life was here before us. If it weren't for experience with other loved ones, we would scarcely believe that life continues after us. We are so wrapped up in our own time and moment that your unfolding plan for all of humankind seems secondary to our individual moments. You keep telling us that more is coming, just as more has been, than we can ever know or imagine. You keep telling us that we are part of God's work, partners with you in the story of love, and that our lifetimes are prime times, the only times, to be about being your person in the flesh with other persons in the flesh. We keep looking for that time when all of this is over, but you keep us focused on the task that is ours to do for one another now.

So, Lord, now we are at your tomb and thinking about our own. Now we have to sneak a peek into the next chapter of your life if we are going to be able to bear the gloom. From whatever spot our remains are set, you will be there with resurrection words, telling us to get up and to come with you. No death has ever been able to stay death in your presence. Lazarus, the widow's son, Jairus' daughter: you brought them all back to life. And you will do the same for us, too.

We give you thanks for Joseph of Arimathea and Nicodemus, who risked their secret love of you on this day of your dying. We give thanks for all who love you secretly for fear of life or persecution. We thank you that you are able to infiltrate every world court, every meeting room, every chamber where decisions are made and note all acts of love done on your behalf. Thank you for making their secret work known.

Lord Jesus, for the work that is ours yet to do, we give you thanks. For moments of service to others, we give you thanks. For letting us *do* love here and now, we give you thanks. May your tomb be a hopeful reminder to expect more to come, so that we do not despair. Be our God, so that all our days will be important ones for you and for us. Amen.

71. WALKING AWAY BEWILDERED

John 20:1-10

Early on the first day of the week, while it was still dark, Mary Magdalene came to the tomb and saw that the stone had been removed from the tomb. So she ran and went to Simon Peter and the other disciple, the one whom Jesus loved, and said to them, "They have taken the Lord out of the tomb, and we do not know where they have laid him." Then Peter and the other disciple set out and went toward the tomb. The two were running together, but the other disciple outran Peter and reached the tomb first. He bent down to look in and saw the linen wrappings lying there, but he did not go in. Then Simon Peter came, following him, and went into the tomb. He saw the linen wrappings lying there, and the cloth that had been on Jesus' head, not lying with the linen wrappings but rolled up in a place by itself. Then the other disciple, who reached the tomb first, also went in, and he saw and believed; for as yet they did not understand the scripture, that he must rise from the dead. Then the disciples returned to their homes.

COMMENTARY

The race to the tomb on that early morning between Peter and "the other disciple" (probably John, the author of this Gospel) must have been a delightful sight for God the Father to witness. What a surprise was in store for them, but the empty tomb alone does not create faith or knowledge. They left bewildered, and Mary stayed behind, not knowing what to think. It would take something far more soul-wrenching than the physical evidence to make them believers again.

PRAYER 71

Lord Jesus, how we have looked at the physical evidence of the empty tomb for proof adequate to bring us to faith. We have noted every detail about the linens. If your body had been stolen, doubtlessly it would have been stolen with the linens wrapped around it. We like the fact that the linen that had been around your head was rolled up and placed aside, as though one was dressing in the morning, and putting away one's pajamas — no hurry, just routine. We like to think that you were quite casual about the time and not worried about being seen. You, the Light of the World, would need no artificial light to dress by.

Sometimes, Lord, we like it to be more dramatic. We want to see the finger of God roll the heavy rock back, or explode it with a snap. We want to see the guards terrorized and thunderstruck, groveling on the ground as you emerge radiantly from the tomb, in brilliant white and light. We want to see the angels hovering about your every step, with a chorus of heavenly hosts singing magnificent alleluias. Lord, you need this event choreographed better than two breathless men racing to a dark, dank tomb, because of a frantic report from Mary Magdalene, and then going home in bewilderment.

So often, Lord, we are that woman and those men who went to the tomb to see what they could see. We, like they, are curious about you. What's going on? What are you up to now? Why are those linens rolled up in an orderly way? What happened to your body? Lord, if they had known the half of it, they would have run *from* the tomb as well as to it. They would have run either in fear or in joy, but they would have run. Because they didn't know what had happened, Mary lingered, and the disciples walked away. They simply went home.

Lord, how many times have we approached your empty tomb, only to walk away bewildered? We are drawn to it in the hope of "having an experience," or securing a faith, but we walk away untouched, unmoved, with no overwhelming sense of your presence or new sense of enlightenment. We peer into the dark, we note the evidence, and our minds nod a type of assent, but like Moses, peering into the promised land from Mount Nebo, we don't seem to have been granted permission to enter. We sense the glory of the occasion, and the transcendent implications, but we are denied a rousing entrance to this divine moment, a cataclysmic event, while all the time others are shaming us for our apparent lack of faith. "Just believe," they counsel us. "Just let go." "Just accept Jesus as personal Lord and Savior," but no amount of effort on our part lets us march to the drumbeat of choreographed ecstasy. It is a matter of honesty not to force our own conversions. You must do it, or it doesn't matter.

We see what the empty tomb means, Lord. The world can never be the same again. Yet some of us do not have personalities that let that knowledge be high public emotion. As we walk in life, as the disciples walked away from the empty tomb, we are pondering mightily. We know that something inexplicable has happened. We know that it has happened for us. We see a new promised land, as surely as Moses saw the old. We see you as much more than a momentary commitment or a day of salvation. You do not let all of us have a glorious emotional conversion, but you convert us nonetheless. You work on us constantly. You do not stop with showing us the simple sight of an empty tomb with discarded linen cloths. You keep coming at us. You keep coming to us. We see that we are your important people, too. We see that you have blessed inheritors of the promised land on both sides of the River Jordan. As you did for Moses on the day of Transfiguration, by grace you will bring us to the other side. You do not love us less, simply because you grace us differently.

Lord Jesus, King, it is resurrection alone, resurrection alone, that is our hope. However you prefer to show us the Kingdom, you will do it gracefully, and you will leave no one out whom you have chosen. Thank you, Lord, for making some of us wait for the fuller experience. The painful waiting is tolerable only because we are not waiting alone. Amen.

72. NAME CALLING

John 20:11-18

But Mary stood weeping outside the tomb. As she wept, she bent over to look into the tomb; and she saw two angels in white, sitting where the body of Jesus had been lying, one at the head and the other at the feet. They said to her, "Woman, why are you weeping?" She said to them, "They have taken away my Lord, and I do not know where they have laid him." When she had said this, she turned around and saw Jesus standing there, but she did not know that it was Jesus. Jesus said to her, "Woman, why are you weeping? Whom are you looking for?" Supposing him to be the gardener, she said to him, "Sir, if you have carried him away, tell me where you have laid him, and I will take him away." Jesus said to her, "Mary!" She turned and said to him in Hebrew, "Rabbouni!" (which means Teacher). Jesus said to her, "Do not hold on to me, because I have not yet ascended to the Father. But go to my brothers and say to them, 'I am ascending to my Father and your Father, to my God and your God.'" Mary Magdalene went and announced to the disciples, "I have seen the Lord," and she told them that he had said these things to her.

COMMENTARY

That Mary could mistake Jesus for a gardener (unless she did not look up to see Jesus' face) is a fascinating matter, with profound implications for the appearance of the body after resurrection. Nevertheless, it was the calling of her name that revealed Jesus' identity.

That Mary could not yet touch Jesus, until he had ascended to the Father, is also a mystery. However, the most amazing words, besides Jesus' revealing himself by the calling of Mary's name, are the two questions he asks, not only of her, but of all people: "Why are you weeping? Whom are you looking for?"

PRAYER 72

Lord Jesus, your first words to Mary, fresh back from the grave, were neither about yourself nor your ordeal, but about her. How could you hold back your emotions? When we have big news, we blurt it out. Any one of us would have gone into a great big display of, "It's me, I'm back, I'm okay, let me tell you about every detail about what it's like to die, and how the resurrection happens, and who I saw, and how I and the Father 'did it.' "

You do none of this. It's as though Mary were more important than your recent victory. It's as though you were casual about this rolling over of history from B.C. to A.D. And what are you doing there at the cemetery? Surely, Jesus, you had better places to be that Sunday morning. A visit to Pilate would be a good start. A few priestly visits wouldn't hurt.

It was just the two of you, Lord, for a moment, with the exchange of names: "Mary!" "Rabbouni!" You were two people calling the other's name, as though nothing had changed; as though you could still love each other; as though death had not separated you forever; as though the two angels standing by were incidental.

Jesus, according to John, you began your ministry with a question to two of John the Baptist's disciples: "What are you looking for?" Now you ask Mary, "Whom are you looking for?" First you asked about her tears, but the second question implied that the tears weren't necessary, that you were there, and that the cause of her grief was gone because you were back. Are these duplicated questions a coincidence, Lord? Is "Whom are you looking for?" really the one question we ought always be asking ourselves? So cleverly you change the "What" to a "Whom." You know that no *thing* is worth looking for. Only you, as person, as God, as Savior, as example, as "Who" can satisfy the most crucial longing of our hearts.

Lord, you asked the question in a cemetery where we all have painful memories. You ask, "Whom are you looking for?" as your first question to a human being after the resurrection. We are there among the dead, in the cemetery, but you are alive and asking tough questions. You don't give us a chance to get maudlin with you, to tell you our needs, our losses, or even our fears about you. You simply ask: "Whom, what, are you looking for?"

If we try to answer that question in your presence, Lord, we are going to have to be more honest than we want to be. You read our minds every time we pretend to be more religious than we really are. You know we are almost always looking for the wrong things, the easy way, and when we pretend it is otherwise, you remind us that you are not only listening to our answer, but you already know our right answer.

Lord, you know that our hearts are set in a direction away from you, and we feel no compulsion to give an account of what we've gone after with our lives. This query from you, in your presence, in the cemetery, provokes more confession than answer, more apology than spirituality for the things of God. We have not been able to cut through all our baggage, like Mary, and greet you with joy and excitement: "Rabbouni! Master! Jesus! Yes, yes, yes!" If it is you asking the question, you are alive! All our fears and all our losses are temporary. All of our worries are needless. All of our questions are answered by life, your life, more life, made new and made forever.

Lord, Mary got excited. She was the first one sent by you with news after your resurrection. You told her to talk about your Ascension, but all she could say was, "I have seen the Lord." You sent her to the disciples with one message, but her joy made her say, "I have seen the Lord." Now we, your disciples, wait for our turn to see if the message is true, to see if you will greet us as personally as you did her. Come, resurrected Lord Jesus, come and call us by name. Amen.

73. THE GOOD NEWS OF FORGIVENESS

John 20:19-23

When it was evening on that day, the first day of the week, and the doors of the house where the disciples had met were locked for fear of the Jews, Jesus came and stood among them and said, "Peace be with you." After he said this, he showed them his hands and his side. Then the disciples rejoiced when they saw the Lord. Jesus said to them, again, "Peace be with you. As the Father has sent me, so I send you." When he had said this, he breathed on them and said to them, "Receive the Holy Spirit. If you forgive the sins of any, they are forgiven them; if you retain the sins of any, they are retained."

COMMENTARY

Jesus twice begins his message to the disciples with the word "Peace." He knows that the very sight of him, alive again, would be a terrifying experience unless he calmed them. He was telling them that wherever he is, there is nothing to fear.

The first thing Jesus does with the disciples, after the rejoicing and the extension of peace, is to "send" them, as he was sent from the Father. He wastes little time talking over old times. They are to be sent, but not alone, for immediately he breathes on them so that they may receive the Holy Spirit, who has the power to forgive sins. They will be sent with power. They will arrive wherever they go with the awesome power of forgiveness.

PRAYER 73

Lord Jesus Christ, it is not for the sake of forgiveness that most of us are interested in you, even though that is what you sent the first disciples out to do. We hardly feel the need for that much forgiveness. Those who tell us that is part of the problem sound like doomers and gloomers. We have mostly decided that guilt is not healthy, so we don't take sin on our backs anymore. We want evangelists coming to us with better promises, more interesting offers, flashier promotions than "forgiveness."

Lord, send the person to us who has a message of love. Send someone telling us about the end of our enemy "death." Send another with words about your constant presence, but don't, Lord, send someone with words about forgiveness, not if you expect a response.

Lord, the truth of the matter is that we feel pretty good about ourselves. We can easily admit to being sinful, but we do it without much shame. Our confession is mainly a matter-of-fact admission of the human situation, but most of us don't really "feel bad" about it. It's the way we are. It's the way you made us, almost.

We, your people, have a tough time putting our sin and your cross together, Jesus. We don't really believe that it was our sin that caused your death, except as "a way of speaking." We know that you died because of sin generally, but not specifically. Surely you understand that we are glad that you died for sin and sinners, but that is somehow different from our behavior, our lack of focus on you, our self-centeredness causing your death. No one on earth is in a position to judge us, Lord. We know that anyone who wants to throw stones at others lives in a glass house, too. We will accept no prophet, no pastor, no persons with lips dripping with guilt. Self-esteem is essential, Lord Jesus, and all this talk about sin and forgiveness is not conducive to mental health.

Lord, we know, even as we pray this prayer, that our defensiveness against needing forgiveness is proof positive that sin has us clenched in its grip. Although we know that this prayer is mostly a lie, we must feel this way about sin if we are to escape self-effacing, old-fashioned piety, Victorian principles, and basic hypocrisy. We know that we cannot list all of our sins. Their numbers are legion, and to confess them all would only depress us and probably bore you. Finding the good news in forgiveness is hard. Instead of dwelling on your goodness we brood morbidly upon our own situation. We dwell upon the deed, even after confessing it, but not upon your goodness, your elimination from your memory of our wrongdoing. We think that we must somehow explain to you why we did what we did, while all the time you are saying, "I know, child of God, about the why of your sin, and I'm sorry that you did it, too. Don't do it again. I don't like it and neither do you.

Now, if we are going to work well together today and tomorrow, you must believe that I've forgotten all about your sin. You must let it go. You must not keep bringing it up. It distracts us both. Believe me. I've taken care of it. I don't have to forgive it twice. It's gone. Over. Done with. Peace."

Lord, say, "Peace," to us with a word of forgiveness. Say it again and again, until we hear it spoken by you with our names attached. Say, "Peace," Lord, to us, as you did to your disciples, even before they said, "I'm sorry." Come to us with open arms as you did to those who were hiding during your dying. Give us a disciple's faith to hear and accept both you and your forgiveness. Come to us, Lord Jesus, and say, "Peace." Amen.

74. MESSIAH

John 20:24-29

But Thomas (who was called the Twin), one of the twelve, was not with them when Jesus came. So the other disciples told him, "We have seen the Lord." But he said to them, "Unless I see the mark of the nails in his hands, and put my finger in the mark of the nails and my hand in his side, I will not believe."

A week later his disciples were again in the house, and Thomas was with them. Although the doors were shut, Jesus came and stood among them and said, "Peace be with you." Then he said to Thomas, "Put your finger here and see my hands. Reach out your hand and put it in my side. Do not doubt but believe." Thomas answered him, "My Lord and my God!" Jesus said to him, "Have you believed because you have seen me? Blessed are those who have not seen and yet have come to believe."

COMMENTARY

Thomas is a true comfort to all of us who doubt. He knew that the place to be, even with his doubt, was with the believers, with those who had seen the Lord. All of us can readily identify and sympathize with Thomas. His declaration of faith in Jesus as the Messiah is the goal of our lives, too.

PRAYER 74

Lord Jesus, thank you for picking Thomas as one of your disciples. His doubt is so much a part of each of us that we understand his reluctance to believe that you were back for good. It probably isn't fair to him to be primarily remembered as the one who doubted, but he represents all of us who were absent from that first gathering of the faithful.

Lord, we give you thanks for Thomas. He is like us today. We know what it's like to feel left out. Like him, we don't want to believe that you are there, among the gathered, when we are not — talking, laughing, living, remembering. Like him, we want it all to happen when we are present. We don't want to be dependent upon witnesses. We especially don't want to be gullible. We want to see you, but not as some sort of imaginary being, or some sort of emotional high. We, like Thomas, want to tell those who are so sure of your presence, "Unless I see your wounded hands and side, forget it."

Lord, Thomas felt left out. We don't know why he couldn't be with them that night. Perhaps he had work to do. It doesn't matter. But, Lord, for you to come among them when he wasn't there had to hurt him deeply. He had to feel unimportant. He had to feel a sadness within, a regret, a longing so deep that all he could do was doubt. So we are glad that he said what he said. He said what we would say, but we are especially pleased that his words were remembered by delighted disciples, knowing within that you wouldn't let him fret for long. They had to view Thomas and his doubt with a loving smile.

Lord, you call those who believe without seeing "blessed." You are talking about us, but we don't always feel so blessed. Sometimes we would trade in a little of our blessedness for a clearer glimpse of your presence. Sometimes we want more than another's witness about you. Sometimes that smile on another's face, who claims to know you, looks more like a smirk than love. Knowing our own weaknesses, it is hard to see you in the weaknesses of others. It is hard to believe that they have an understanding of you that we don't yet have. And yes, it is very hard to believe that someday, someone may even see you in one of us!

Lord, all of the disciples saw you. None of them had to believe without seeing, as we do. All of them, sooner or later, were eyewitnesses. We get jealous of them, Lord, until the cost of seeing you is remembered. Almost all of them were martyred for you, and those that weren't probably were willing to be. They paid a dear price for being an eyewitness. As the years passed, and danger was near, they probably wanted to hide from you as we do, saying, "I'm not sure ... I don't remember it exactly ... It was a long time ago." You were not with them in the flesh for the rest of their days upon earth. In the end, all they had were memories and your Holy Spirit. In the end, they had to die with faith alone as companion.

Lord, Thomas said it all when he said, "My Lord and my God!" Not only were you worthy of service as Lord, you were worthy of worship as God. He knew you were the Messiah. He had the wisdom to undo his doubt with praise. He made no apology, just song. He chased shame away with joy. He gave you the honor and the glory and the power and swallowed his pride. He revealed your true identity to the world. He was first to name you Messiah.

Thank you, Lord, for Thomas and his doubt. Thank you for letting him be the one to name you rightly. May we also, despite our doubt, know you as Jesus the Christ, Messiah, the Savior of the world. Amen.

75. A THANK YOU FOR JOHN

John 20:30, 31

Now Jesus did many other signs in the presence of his disciples, which are not written in this book. But these are written so that you may come to believe that Jesus is the Messiah, the Son of God, and that through believing you may have life in his name.

COMMENTARY

Normally, we would expect to see the purpose of a book at its beginning, not buried almost at the end. John's motives are purer than pure. His labor in writing this Gospel is not for fame or gain, not just for the Gospel's sake, but for us, that we may believe.

PRAYER 75

Thank you, Lord, for John. His modesty is overcome by his passion for you in every passage. He loved you more dearly than his own life. He poured out his soul into the words given him by the Spirit to write. He showed no doubt in you ever. He took your mother home. He was there at the last supper, at the crucifixion, at the empty tomb, and in the upper room. He never missed a step. He knew where to expect you next.

Lord, thank you for his purity of heart. He willed one thing: to tell your story. He found in life what we are looking for — not a cause, but a person. He loved you, Lord Jesus, and in that loving, he wanted us to know you as he did. He had no selfishness in his love. He knew that you were love enough for all of us to love completely, without your love diminishing.

Thank you, Lord, for his example of devotion. Thank you for using him to accomplish the task of bringing us to faith. Thank you for John. Amen.

76. WHEN OTHERS ARE AROUND

John 21:1-14

After these things Jesus showed himself again to the disciples by the Sea of Tiberias; and he showed himself in this way. Gathered there together were Simon Peter, Thomas called the Twin, Nathanael of Cana in Galilee, the sons of Zebedee, and two others of his disciples. Simon Peter said to them, "I am going fishing." They went out and got into the boat, but that night they caught nothing.

Just after daybreak, Jesus stood on the beach; but the disciples did not know that it was Jesus. Jesus said to them, "Children, you have no fish, have you?" They answered him, "No." He said to them, "Cast the net to the right side of the boat, and you will find some." So they cast it, and now they were not able to haul it in because there were so many fish. That disciple whom Jesus loved said to Peter, "It is the Lord!" When Simon Peter heard that it was the Lord, he put on some clothes, for he was naked, and jumped into the sea. But the other disciples came in the boat, dragging the net full of fish, for they were not far from the land, only about a hundred yards off.

When they had gone ashore, they saw a charcoal fire there, with fish on it, and some bread. Jesus said to them, "Bring some of the fish that you have just caught." So Simon Peter went aboard and hauled the net ashore, full of large fish, a hundred fifty-three of them; and though there were so many, the net was not torn. Jesus said to them, "Come and have breakfast." Now none of the disciples dared to ask him, "Who are you?" because they knew it was the Lord. Jesus came and took the bread and gave it to them, and did the same with the fish. This was now the third time that Jesus appeared to the disciples after he was raised from the dead.

COMMENTARY

Simon Peter is all fisherman. It was his idea to go fishing, but it was his fearless leaping into the sea at the sight of Jesus and his hauling aboard the net full of fishes that delight us.

Meanwhile, Jesus was fixing breakfast for all of them over a charcoal fire. This appearance, like the others, was done simply and without fanfare. There is no prelude, no preparatory worship service, no sermon. It was natural and at Jesus' initiative.

PRAYER 76

Lord Jesus Christ, we often try to make you come to us through our own elaborate preparations. Sometimes we pretend we are in the spirit with you when we are not; sometimes we deny you are with us in simplicity, when you are. You like to surprise us. Breakfast on the beach had to be a wonderful surprise for the disciples.

Lord Jesus, unless you come to us we will never see you. We can do all the right things, go to all the right places, say all the right words, but unless you decide to use the moment, it is all for nothing. The best we can do is to be open to your coming. We cannot manipulate you, try though we might. You will not be forced. You will come with surprise when you come, when we least expect it. You will come and go, sometimes, before we even know it is you.

Lord Jesus, we yearn for encounters with you. We want to spend intimate time with you, talking about our relationship. We almost want to be your romantic lover, on the beach, strolling arm in arm, as though the world could pass us by and it wouldn't matter. When we are with you, we tend to forget the others. We keep wanting to make you our own, to possess you, to have you exclusively. We forget your love for the whole human family, so you keep coming to us when others are around. You keep coming to us through others. You make sure that your intention and our experience cannot be misunderstood. You do not scorn the presence of other believers, even when saying lovely things to us alone.

We are glad that Peter wasn't alone in the boat the morning you fixed breakfast. We are glad that it was another on board who recognized you first. We are glad that you called out to all of them to come to shore for breakfast, and not just Peter. You keep including us, even when we are not as flashy as the man called Peter. You feed us all, not just the one target for personal conversation. You make us all special.

Lord, we don't know how you knew there were fish on one side of the boat, but not the other. After all, Peter was the fisherman, not you! He should have known. It doesn't matter. "The earth is yours and the fullness thereof."

You can do whatever you want to do, on earth and off, and you can do it far better than we can do it. You are the expert in all things, but you still give us the pleasure of hauling it in and counting the fish.

Lord, we look forward to the morning that you awake us with words similar to "Come and have breakfast." We have placed our hope in your standing over our graves, saying, "Wake up and come with me." We yearn for the morning that never ends, the day of great reunion, the shedding of these earth bodies to don one like yours, fit for eternal life. We want to live forever, not for life's sake, but for your sake. We want to be your friend forever, doing the will of our heavenly Father. Amen.

77. ONE ON ONE

John 21:15-19

When they had finished breakfast, Jesus said to Simon Peter, "Simon son of John, do you love me more than these?" He said to him, "Yes, Lord; you know that I love you." Jesus said to him, "Feed my lambs." A second time he said to him, "Simon son of John, do you love me?" He said to him, "Yes, Lord; you know that I love you." Jesus said to him, "Tend my sheep." He said to him the third time, "Simon son of John, do you love me?" Peter felt hurt because he said to him the third time, "Do you love me?" And he said to him, "Lord, you know everything; you know that I love you." Jesus said to him, "Feed my sheep. Very truly, I tell you, when you were younger, you used to fasten your own belt and to go wherever you wished. But when you grow old, you will stretch out your hands, and someone else will fasten a belt around you and take you where you do not wish to go." (He said this to indicate the kind of death by which he would glorify God.) After this he said to him, "Follow me."

COMMENTARY

Jesus begins every one of his three questions to Peter with the calling of his name. Like Mary at the empty tomb, the calling of his name made him know it was one on one.

Peter could not help but recall that he had denied Jesus three times. This threefold questioning of him was designed to never let him forget that God knew his name, and he was never to betray God again. It may have grieved Peter for a season, but through the ordeal he became a seasoning himself, a salt, an inspiration for the rest of us, even as they tightened the promised belt around him and led him to a martyr's death.

As Jesus pulled Peter gently away from his friends, in order that his primary loyalty might be established forever, he did it by asking him about his loves. "Do you love me more than these?" Jesus asked, and Peter had to compare his love for the friends of this world to the love he had for Christ.

Jesus' commands to Peter are for our sake: "Feed my lambs. Tend my sheep. Feed my sheep." In a way, Peter is expendable, as are any of us individually, because Jesus can, and will, resurrect us. But until that day, our witness of faithfulness in the midst of adversity is grist for the mill of Christian faith.

PRAYER 77

Lord Jesus Christ, three times you called Peter by name, three times, formally, at length, before asking him anything. You named him, and he could never deny that you knew him inside and out, intimately, lovingly.

Did Peter know that hearing his name on your lips, Lord, meant that he was being called to die to this world? Probably so. The two of you were on the wrestler's mat, and you would win, because you are who you are. You are irresistible when you call our names.

Lord, sometimes we like to be incognito. We like to get lost in the crowd and have no demands placed upon us. If you know our names, how can we hide from your presence, even for a moment's worth of privacy? If we want to take a moment away from being your person, but you know our name, how can we ever be free from your gaze, free from your presence, free from responsibility for the next chore? You give us no rest. You know how to find us in our most secret places. You come in through our hearts and minds, and no place is secure from your calling.

We could die serving you, Lord, and who would care? Like Peter, we could be called upon to give up not only our fishing boats and friends and leisure, but also our lives; and what would we do for you without them?

It is hard to believe that we are expendable to you. It is hard to believe that death for the sake of love is the only message that most of the world can hear. So long as it's your death, okay, but not ours. We have no desire to be martyrs. We like the thought of a quiet and peaceable life. We would rather go fishing with Peter.

Lord, you pulled Peter away from his nets. You sent him out with the knowledge that he, himself, was caught. You knew his name, and he could not get away.

In the end, Lord, that had to be the most wonderful of all the facts of his life. You gave him singularity. You marked him with your cross and you called him by name. Then, and only then, did you give him work to do.

Lord, you know my name. You know our names. We cannot pretend it is otherwise. First you call us by name, ask us about our first love, then you send us. You mark us with your cross, and at baptism you adopt us. Once we were no one. Now we are someone. Now we are your sent followers. Amen.

78. WE WILL

John 21:20-25
Peter turned and saw the disciple whom Jesus loved following them; he was the one who had reclined next to Jesus at the supper and had said, "Lord, who is it that is going to betray you?" When Peter saw him, he said to Jesus, "Lord, what about him?" Jesus said to him, "If it is my will that he remain until I come, what is that to you? Follow me!" So the rumor spread in the community that this disciple would not die. Yet Jesus did not say to him that he would not die, but "If it is my will that he remain until I come, what is that to you?"

This is the disciple who is testifying to these things and has written them, and we know that his testimony is true. But there are also many other things that Jesus did; if every one of them were written down, I suppose that the world itself could not contain the books that would be written.

COMMENTARY

Now that Jesus had Peter's commitment, that commitment would cost Peter his life. He couldn't help but look back, wistfully perhaps, and see John following them. Peter just had to know, "What about him? Does he have to die too?"

Rumors spread quickly about the implications of Jesus' words about John, so John sets the record straight about what Jesus said regarding his own death. John understood Jesus to be saying that all of the future is his business alone. Like the God who said, "I am who I am," Jesus was saying, "I will do what I will do and be what I will be." We don't have to know as much of the future as we think we do. We just have to obey the last command: "Follow me."

PRAYER 78

Lord Jesus, Peter knew how much you loved John, and when he saw him following the two of you, right after you told Peter that he would suffer greatly for you, and die on your behalf, it was a natural question to ask. He wanted to know, "Lord, will there be others who have to give this much? Am I the only one who has to die? Did my betrayal bring this about? Will John, whom you love so dearly, also have to die a cruel death?"

Your answer, Lord, once again took all such speculative matters out of Peter's hands. You would not tell him your plans for John, for Matthew, for James, or for that matter, for us. You simply told Peter what he was to do: "Follow me."

Lord, misery loves company. Persons whose lives are touched by tragedy need real support from others, not just sympathy. Peter wanted to know that his sacrifice was essential, that others would love you as he did, and that others would have to face the pain of the cross, along with him. You gave him no guarantees. You only told him to do what you've told us to do: "Follow me." He could not see what we now know, that all but one of your disciples died a martyr's death, including your beloved John. Your way is so costly. You give us so many opportunities to die too. They may not be as dramatic as crucifixion, but they are painful deaths for us nonetheless, because we are dying to self for the sake of another. You ask us to do it for you.

So, Lord, we will do just that. We have had time to read and learn that millions have followed you through the ages, and found that dying for you for the sake of another was peace indeed. We will have to die to be your child. We understand it, and we will do it, with your help, because to live any other way is to live without peace, to live without you. We do not choose to do this, Lord, but you have commanded us to follow your will.

We will.

Lord, this promise to you is not easily spoken, for behind the words is much uncertainty about our strength and ability to keep our vow. We will need your constant help and presence, as you've promised. But what a journey it will be in community together, your band of disciples for this time. What a different road we will have to travel together. What an adventure it is has already been.

John concludes his book about you, Lord, with thoughts about how many other books would have to be written to tell what you have done on our behalf. Comfort us with the knowledge that we are a part of that written record, with many surprise chapters, unknown to us at this time, but a delight to learn in the world yet to come. Comfort us with the knowledge that we know enough for now. Later, Lord, we will learn it all and tremble at your love.

To you, Lord Jesus, be all mystery and might, as you form our lives on your own potter's wheel. Push us and pull us, spin us, and remold us as necessary, for without your touch, we are but sorry clumps of clay. To your glory, and for your sake, these words are prayed. To your purpose, may our lives be lived. For our sake and the sake of the world, for which you died, give us strength for the battle, until the day of resurrection. Amen.

www.ingramcontent.com/pod-product-compliance
Lightning Source LLC
Chambersburg PA
CBHW070739160426
43192CB00009B/1496